Arguing with Derrida

Arguing with Derrida

Edited by

Simon Glendinning

BLACKWELL
Publishers

Copyright © Blackwell Publishers Ltd 2001

This edition first published 2001

Blackwell Publishers Ltd
108 Cowley Road
Oxford OX4 1JF, UK

Blackwell Publishers Inc
350 Main Street
Malden, Massachusetts 02148, USA

British Library Cataloguing in Publication Data has been applied for

Library of Congress Cataloging in Publication Data has been applied for

ISBN 0–631–22652–4 (pbk)

Typeset by Cambrian Typesetters, Frimley, Surrey

By MPG Books, Bodmin, Cornwall

This book is printed on acid-free paper

Contents

Preface
Simon Glendinning   1

Inheriting 'Philosophy': The Case of Austin and Derrida
Revisited
Simon Glendinning   9

Session One
For the Sake of Argument (Up to a Point)
Geoffrey Bennington   34

Response to Bennington
Jacques Derrida   52

Session Two
Arguing with Derrida
A. W. Moore   57

Response to Moore
Jacques Derrida   83

Session Three
Death and Meaning – Some Questions for Derrida
Thomas Baldwin   89

Response to Baldwin
Jacques Derrida   102

Wittgenstein and Deconstruction
Stephen Mulhall   109

Response to Mulhall
Jacques Derrida   116

The Reading Affair: On Why Philosophy is not "Philosophical"
Through and Through
Darren Sheppard   121

Notes on Contributors   135

Index   137

PREFACE

Arguing with Derrida

This book comprises the edited proceedings of the 1999 *Ratio* conference 'Arguing with Derrida'.[1] Collections such as this normally have a rather uniform and formal appearance. Conference addresses which had been delivered to a responsive and questioning audience are, at the end of the day, dislocated and sealed-up into a standard 'journal article' format. The published remains of a conference thus line up like works of art, or corpses.

Motivated in part by the fact that Derrida responded so fully in each discussion session of the conference, it was decided that on this occasion it would be particularly fitting for the remains of the day to be made available in a more complete and less formal form. However, the text that is published here is not simply a cough-for-cough transcript. In the weeks that followed the conference I did, in fact, produce such a transcript from tape-recordings. But the first thing I discovered was that almost nobody can extemporize in sentences. (Derrida, more experienced than most in this mode, was actually uncannily good, but English is not his first language and there was work to be done there too.) So the text was modified (very little but just enough) to produce something comfortably readable. Where possible the new versions have been shown to the contributors (some of the questioners have not been identified, those who we could identify sometimes altered their remarks a little bit more in their turn – but I kept a watchful eye for any attempts to remove perceived gaffs and errors after the fact), and I think that the text presented here will give readers a very fair impression of the proceedings at the conference.

[1] There are two exceptions here. The first and last essays were not presented (could not have been presented) at the conference. In the light of the conference, the former revisits one of the 'affairs' that forms an important part of its background; namely, Derrida's controversial engagements with the 'ordinary language philosophy' of J. L. Austin. The latter reflects, after the event, on the 'Reading affair' itself and examines the import of some of Derrida's responses to the conference papers. I am grateful to Darren Sheppard for agreeing to undertake the latter project under considerable time pressure, and for producing such a valuable contribution to the proceedings.

As the conference title nicely indicates (and I am grateful to Jonathan Dancy for suggesting it to me) one of my hopes for the day was that the participants would engage with and explore (whether critically or sympathetically or both) arguments and demonstrations in Derrida's work. I make no bones about the fact that I wanted the event to make trouble for those opponents (or, indeed, defenders) of Derrida who believe that he believes that *any* such 'structure' must be a (say) 'logocentric prejudice' to be undermined and avoided. I do not find that view convincing, and I organised the conference with a view to making a step beyond the prevailing, although these days by no means ubiquitous, 'hear-say' reception of his work; a reception which either simply ignores or, in its head-over-heals aggressivity, seemingly willfully distorts, Derrida's (no doubt not-simply-classical) argumentative strategies. I think the conference was successful in that regard. And I would like to take this opportunity to thank the participants, Thomas Baldwin, Geoffrey Bennington, A.W. Moore and Stephen Mulhall, for their crucial part in making it so. Naturally, I want also to express my special thanks and gratitude to Jacques Derrida for the incredible efforts he made both to attend the conference in the first place and in his generous and constructive contributions throughout it.

The constructive potential of such events was underscored in March 2000 when Marian Hobson organized a follow-up conference at Queen Mary and Westfield College, London, with Derrida and the other participants at Reading (with the exception of the unavailable Moore, and with the addition of me as a speaker). For that occasion, Marian Hobson suggested an even more detailed engagement with Derrida's work, asking the participants to restrict their attention to a particular (and preferably short) passage of text. It was an extremely interesting and instructive meeting, not least because some of the themes which began to take shape at Reading were raised again, and raised in a more focused way. The topic I chose to discuss was Derrida's claim that the kind of differential or iterable structure he identifies as internal to language (and not only language) escapes 'the logic of presence'. Because they emerged out of the discussions at the conference, some of the thoughts I developed for that occasion might helpfully preface the proceedings to come.

The kind of claim that I focused on is made very directly and explicitly in a passage in Derrida's *Limited Inc.*[2]

[2] Jacques Derrida, *Limited Inc*, ed. G. Graff (Evanston: Northwestern University Press,

The iterability of an element divides its own identity a priori, even without taking into account that this identity can only determine or delimit itself through differential relations to other elements and hence that it bears the mark of this difference. It is because this iterability is differential, within each individual 'element' as well as between 'elements' . . . that the remainder, although indispensable, is never that of a full or fulfilling presence: it is a differential structure escaping the logic of presence. (Derrida 1988, p. 53)

One of the most detailed arguments in support of this claim can be found in the quasi-Saussurean discussion at the beginning of Derrida's 1968 essay 'Différance' (pp. 4–5).[3] As I see it, the argument runs as follows:

1. Assume that what belongs to sensibility is always the perception of some present sensory data. (For example, assume that what can be 'heard' is always a sound or is composed of sounds or properties of sounds.)
2. Articulate, meaningful speech is, by definition, something which can be heard.
3. For articulate, meaningful speech to be possible, a language must contain a number of discriminably different 'units' (call them 'phonemes'). People must be able to discriminate different phonemes if speech is to function as such.
4. The difference between two phonemes is not itself a sound – not some third sound, not an audible 'something'.
5. Therefore the difference which establishes speech and lets it be heard is inaudible ('in every sense of the word').
6. But since meaningful speech is possible the difference between two phonemes must still be discriminable.
7. Therefore one ought to reject the idea that such discrimination belongs to sensibility.

1988). While Geoffrey Bennington suggests in his contribution to this volume that it is 'a largely mistaken perception' to suppose that Derrida's 'theses...are not properly backed up by argument', the discussion that follows can be fruitfully compared to what he refers to as 'philosophical' attempts to 'improve' (by a kind of castration) Derrida's writings by 'extracting' (like teeth or confessions) arguments set out as 'a sequence of related propositions'. It would be a fascinating project to think through the relation between this 'formal' text and the particulars of Derrida's presentation that I do not pick up on, or elide 'for the sake of argument'.

   [3] Jacques Derrida, *Margins of Philosophy*, trans. A. Bass (Hemel Hempstead: The Harvester Press, 1982)

According to this argument, what is discriminated when one hears an identifiable phoneme *cannot* be reduced to a sound which is simply present in the present. And that is because, as Derrida puts it in the passage quoted above, its 'identity can only determine or delimit itself through differential relations to other elements'. Or again, as Saussure puts it, the basic elements of speech are not substantial positive terms or sound atoms, but only emerge out of, or issue from, a system of phonic differences.

This conclusion entails a denial of the (otherwise quite intuitive) empiricist assumption that what is heard is always and simply sounds or properties of sounds, something fully present in the present; and hence, if acceptable, the argument requires a rejection of the assumption that the discrimination of phonemes 'belongs to sensibility' (ibid., p. 5). At this point in the essay Derrida invites the repetition of the same argument for writing. Graphic differences 'can never be sensed as a full term' either (ibid.). In short, in neither case can we maintain the view that the discrimination of differences which makes possible the apprehension of linguistic signs 'belongs to sensibility'.

In the very next sentence Derrida's discussion begins to mount a challenge not just to every empiricism, but, as it were, to philosophy as such. For he goes on to claim that this 'discrimination of differences' cannot belong to an 'order of intelligibility' either. We cannot conclude, as for example Descartes might have concluded, that the perception of phonemes entails that something is present not to the senses but is ('seen' or 'heard' by) the mind, or the mind's eye or ear.

I do not want to go into the details of this step in Derrida's argument. It draws in part from a wider (and more or less Heideggerian) recognition that human understanding has been interpreted, from Greek times, in terms derived from sensibility, or perhaps better, it draws on the observation that from Greek times sensibility and understanding (perception and conception) have been *the* terms through which human cognition has been interpreted, and *both* are interpreted in terms of the apprehension of something present – in terms that is of the same 'logic of presence'. It is this 'logic' that the claims concerning the differential structure of signs is intended to resist or escape. And so, without examining the independent argument further, we will conclude:

8. One ought also to reject the idea that such discrimination belongs to intelligibility.

With this addition the conclusion of the main argument is as follows:

9. We must let ourselves refer to an order that resists one of the founding oppositions of philosophy.

This resisting order, 'is announced' Derrida says 'in a movement of différance...which belongs neither to the voice nor to writing in the usual sense' (ibid.). This order, I take it, is the organisation that is 'writing' in the *general* sense of that word that Derrida defends in other essays (see, eg. 'Signature Event Context', in Derrida 1988).

With this claim I am making a connection to a whole dimension of the 'movement of *différance*' which I have not mentioned but which is picked out in the quotation I began with in the idea that the iterability of an element 'is differential, within each individual "element" as well as between "elements"'. But, I suggest, even if we hold that idea to one side we can still draw the same basic lesson from the argument I have just rehearsed. Namely, that the condition of *possibility* of the 'presence' of signs in actuality is, at once, the condition of *impossibility* that this presence be reducible to anything simply present in the present.

Here we meet a distinction which, it seems to me, runs throughout many of Derrida's arguments and demonstrations: the distinction between an impossible philosophical ideal and the actual structure and functioning of marks and traces (spoken or written), the latter characterised by a 'logic' which, as Derrida puts it, 'often passes unseen' (Derrida 1988, p. 18) and which is incompatible with those tempting interpretations dominated by a logic of presence.

This distinction, the distinction between the philosophical ideal and the extraordinary actual, is one I think Derrida needs. It is also something I find in Wittgenstein. In order to develop this point, and in order also to highlight a certain difference that this comparison will bring out, I want briefly to look at Wittgenstein's way of drawing the distinction in the *Philosophical Investigations*:[4]

A picture is conjured up which seems to fix the sense *unambiguously*. The actual use, compared with that suggested by the picture, seems like something muddied . . . In the actual use of

[4] Ludwig Wittgenstein, *Philosophical Investigations*, trans. G.E.M. Anscombe (Oxford: Blackwell, 1958)

6   SIMON GLENDINNING

expressions we make detours, we go by side-roads. We see the
straight highway before us, but of course we cannot use it,
because it is permanently closed. (Wittgenstein 1958, §426)

In a part of this remark that I have not reproduced here,
Wittgenstein says that the forms of expression that characterise
the philosophical interpretation of language 'are like pontificals
which we may put on, but cannot do much with'. Nevertheless, in
their light the actual practice of language, the way that takes side-
roads, can readily appear compromised or impure or lacking in
something that we feel they ought, ideally, to have. Wittgenstein
describes this scene as one in which we are held 'captive',
'seduced' by 'false appearances' which our language repeatedly
invites. The concern I want to raise is whether some of the details
of Derrida's thinking are sometimes caught in the glare of this
dissatisfaction with the extraordinary actual.

To see this let us go back to the argument I rehearsed earlier.
In my view that argument gives a convincing case for supposing
that we must 'let ourselves refer to an order that resists the opposition between the sensible and the intelligible'. That is right – or
at least that is right in so far as it requires that we think the 'presence of signs' otherwise than according to a traditional logic of
presence. But there is a detail in this argument which threatens
to problematise far more than a philosophical picture. The detail
is this. Derrida does not just say that the difference which establishes speech and lets it be heard is, *in the terms of traditional philosophy*, inaudible; but rather that it is inaudible 'in every sense of
the word'. But isn't there, in fact, a quite unexceptionable sense
in which it is audible? Equally, Derrida does not just say that the
difference which establishes speech and lets it be heard is, *in the
terms of traditional philosophy*, not intelligible or not understandable; but rather, simply that it cannot belong to intelligibility or
understanding. But isn't there, in fact, a quite unexceptional
sense in which such a difference is something that can be, as one
might say, 'heard with understanding'? Heidegger calls such
hearing that understands 'hearkening' [*Horchen*] and positions it
as 'more primordial' than 'the sensing of tones and the perception of sounds.'[5] Wittgenstein calls it a case of aspect perception
or 'hearing as', and, at least arguably, suggests that everyday

[5] Martin Heidegger, *Being and Time*, trans. J. Macquarrie and E. Robinson (Oxford:
Blackwell, 1962), p. 207.

perception in general just is 'continuous aspect perception' (see Wittgenstein 1968, Part II section xi).

So the difference can be heard. But, yes: it can be heard in a sense that can never be heard by traditional philosophy. And yet, some of the details of Derrida's work suggest that the demonstration of the impossibility of hearing, seeing, understanding, meaning (etc.) anything, *as these are interpreted in philosophy*, means that we never really hear, see, understand or mean anything, at least not 'fully' or not 'properly'. This seems problematic to me. At least the case needs to be made as to why Wittgenstein is wrong to treat philosophical ideals as mere 'pontificals'. There is, I think, a plausibility to Wittgenstein's suggestion that the impossibility of the philosophical ideal, the permanent closure of the straight highway, does nothing to compromise the side-roads we actually take. Thus while both Derrida and Wittgenstein are in agreement concerning the 'inadequacy' of our concepts when compared to the ideal, for Wittgenstein this is clearly an ideal of 'adequacy' that is a kind of (no doubt original and structural) fantasy of our language. Derrida's commitments on this point remain less clear to me. For the purposes of discussion I will identify two kinds of response to the philosophical idealization of concepts. I will leave them unattributed and mean to imply that I really do not know what Derrida will want to say, but sometimes hear him saying something like the first, and sometimes (like Wittgenstein) something like the second:

Either:

a) There are no concepts, no rigorous concepts – and only for this reason can signs function

Or:

b) That notion of a concept is a philosophical construction – and our language, our concepts can and must function without it.

Both of these views accepts that our words and concepts can and do function, and can do so not *despite* the fact that the straight-highway is closed, but *on condition* of its closure. So my question is not why Derrida treats philosophical ideals as in need of deconstruction, but, rather, why he seems sometimes to treat the actual structure he so carefully analyses as *also* a falling short of, or interruption of, a movement towards an ideal; as if we *do* take the straight highway – but (to use the subtitle of

Bennington's contribution to this volume) always only 'up to a point'. This is one issue about which, thankfully, I am still arguing with Derrida.

Simon Glendinning
The University of Reading

INHERITING 'PHILOSOPHY':
THE CASE OF AUSTIN AND DERRIDA REVISITED

Simon Glendinning

In his contribution to this volume A.W. Moore mentions that I had encouraged him to resist casting his discussion of Derrida's work in terms of a contrast between Derrida's 'style' and that of 'analytical philosophy'. My main worry was that this contrast might too readily be taken by his readers to be informed by, or even be an instance of, the more general contrast between analytical and continental philosophy. And in my view (a view I take to be shared by both Moore and Derrida)[1] that general distinction is both too vague (Can anyone seriously maintain that drawing this distinction meets the 'accepted standards of clarity and rigour' which should characterise philosophical inquiry?)[2] and too overdetermined (The supposition of division is not an impartial assessment and its description carries an irreducibly evaluative accent.) to be remotely helpful.

This is not to say that I suppose the distinction between analytical and continental philosophy to be of no philosophical significance whatsoever. Indeed, certain philosophical differences between the thinking and teaching in the current philosophical culture, differences which might well be summarised under these titles, are readily apparent – as evidenced, for example, in bibliographies and reading lists. What is at issue at this level is something

---

[1] Moore chose to style his own (no doubt also 'analytical') approach as 'conceptual philosophy' in order to mark, on the one hand, that 'analytic philosophy embraces more than what I was calling conceptual philosophy' and, on the other hand, that 'there may be a lack of fit in the other direction as well. That is, there may be things that deserve to be called conceptual philosophy that don't count as analytic philosophy' (Moore, p. 76). Derrida seemed keen to welcome this point and was seriously willing to risk representing what he tries to do as conceptual philosophy too. In relation to the topic of this paper it is significant that Derrida went on to add that this complicates the standard picture of a clear division between two 'fronts': 'Despite a number of appearances, my "style" has something essential to do with a motivation that one also finds in analytic philosophy, in conceptual philosophy. From that point of view, then, there are no fronts here. I am, rather, on the side of conceptual philosophy' (Derrida, p. 84).

[2] This is a (cheeky) reference to the infamous letter to *The Times* objecting to the proposal to award Derrida an honorary degree from Cambridge University in 1992. See Barry Smith et. al., 'Derrida Degree: A Question of Honour', *The Times* (London), Saturday, May 9, 1992.

like a division within what is philosophically 'new' which is defined, at least in part, by differing views of pertinence and importance in what gets figured as 'old'. That is, the division, conceived as a philosophical separation, is a division of tradition or of inheritance. On this understanding, however, if we wish to distinguish analytical and continental philosophy as 'different ways of going on', we must be ready to read this as referring, in the first instance, not to differing positions or methods, but to different ways of going *on*, of continuing doing 'philosophy'; to the possession of a philosophical past.

Bernard Williams captures a typical 'analytical' avowal of this thought when he observes that 'it is a feature of our time that the resources of philosophical writing typically available to analytical philosophy should present themselves so strongly as the responsible way of going on, the most convincing expression of a philosopher's claim on people's attention.' (Williams 1996, p. 27) Before we conclude from this that being-an-heir to 'philosophy' can be reduced to the reception of something available, a given which presents itself strongly, we should note that Williams is giving voice to a position for which the division of inheritance has already been drawn: 'the resources available to analytical philosophy' just are what it cites as its typical resources. The novel 'feature of our time' is that, *in view of a larger stock*, analytical philosophy evinces little or no concern about its limits. In question, then, is not the passive acquisition of a forceful fragment of what is available, but, relatively confident acts of endorsement, what one might call the 'countersigning' of a particular way of going on. The internecine aspects evident within the current philosophical culture would then flow from the fact that one would see the same confidence on the other side. And so the scene is one in which, as Stanley Cavell has put it, both sides have 'become ludicrous to one another' (Cavell 1994, p. 64).

All this seems to me undeniable. And yet – *none of it helps*. For at the level of actually reading and interpreting philosophical texts, at the level in which positions or methods are precisely what concerns us, the distinction is virtually insignificant. Or rather its significance at that point lies in its dubious power to *replace* actually reading and interpreting philosophical texts. As Michael Dummett discovered when reading Husserl (for the first time, as it were, without skipping), and found (to his surprise) how close Husserl really was to Frege, matters can look very different when one turns one's attention to the details of argument and their presuppositions.³ There, where acts of inheritance or disinheritance take place *within* the productive procedures of the text itself, the 'reservoir of arguments' to which particular thinkers are indebted are often more subtle, more subterranean and more mobile 'across the divide' than the polemical battle-cries of philosophical affiliation would suggest.⁴

So in this paper, in order to set the scene for my wish to stage a new meeting between Derrida and what Geoffrey Bennington, in his contribution, playfully called 'the (real) philosophers', I will not be trying to get to the bottom of the analytical/continental division, but to make a start in working without it. My topic is one in which the problematic of inheritance is itself a central and inescapable issue; namely, Derrida's controversial reading of J.L. Austin's theory of performative utterances. The reason why the meeting of 'deconstruction' and 'ordinary language philosophy' is particularly congenial to my aim is that, despite obvious expectations to the contrary, its basic themes suggest that the idea of a distinction between analytical and continental philosophy clouds rather than clarifies what is at stake in the 'ways of going on' which are our contemporary modes of being-an-heir to 'philosophy'.

To some extent the acceptability of this conclusion will presume that the themes being discussed generalise in a fruitful way beyond the Austin/Derrida debate. I do not pretend that this can be proved, but I hope to offer a presentation which gives credence to its plausibility. The discussion falls into three parts. Beginning with Bernard Williams' characterisation of analytical philosophy in terms of its 'plain style', a more inclusive net will be considered by exploring certain parallels between Derrida's and Austin's criticisms of a style of thinking they are both willing to call, simply, 'philosophy' (section I). In the light of this comparison, a re-appraisal of Derrida's reading of Austin is presented (sections II, III and IV). The aim of these sections is to show that Austin's own 'way of going on' is, in a particularly pointed respect, open to just the kind of criticism that he (Austin) levels at 'philosophy'. Finally, I show how this presentation of the case of Austin and Derrida furnishes an approach to contemporary philosophy in general

---

³ See Dummett (1996, p. 14).
⁴ The reservoir image comes from Derrida (1988, p. 36), although, as we shall see, the idea that one's philosophical inheritance is often 'unconscious' and 'unwitting' is a typically Austinian thought too (see, Austin 1980, p. 12).

that is centred not on its plainness (or obscurity) of style but its
ways of styling the plain (section V).

I

No-one engaged in philosophy today can remain oblivious to the
presence and force of the division between analytical and continental philosophy. But what kind of division is this? Bernard
Williams has argued that what is at issue in labelling a work by one
of these titles is a matter not so much of its content but of its style.[5]
For example, he claims that analytical philosophy can be distinguished 'from other contemporary philosophy' by the fact that it
tries to employ 'moderately plain speech' (Williams 1985,
Preface). This plain style is, he accepts, still a style – and hence
'must to some extent determine subject matter' (*ibid.*) – but, he
supposes, it has the distinctive virtue of affording the kind of clarity and accuracy possessed by the sciences.

While Williams is convinced that this virtue is indeed a virtue,
he sees no advantage to attempts to make philosophy simply look
like a science. Indeed, he is ruefully sure that certain aspects of
his own work 'are obscure because I have tried to make them
clear' (*ibid.*). This is much more than a prefatory acknowledgement of the personal provenance of error. It is to question
whether the minimally expressive style of the sciences, and their
quest for theoretical simplicity, can do justice to the phenomena
that philosophy (and, in Williams' view, especially moral philosophy) takes as its subject matter. In short, it raises the question
whether the plain style with its supposedly clear content can
harbour its own lack of clarity concerning its way of going on.

But how much, and so how worryingly? In response to
complaints about the distinctively not-so-plain style of his own
work, Derrida defends a characteristically radical view of the
merits of conceiving clarity in terms of theoretical simplicity:

> These things are difficult, I admit; their formulation can be
> disconcerting. But would there be so many problems and misun-
> derstandings without this complexity? One shouldn't complicate
> things for the pleasure of complicating, but one should also
> never simplify or pretend to be sure of such simplicity where

---

[5] We should note that in Williams' view these titles are not only 'obscure' and 'misleading' but involve a ridiculous cross-classification, 'rather as though one divided cars into
front-wheel drive and Japanese' (Williams 1996, p. 25).

there is none. If things were simple word would have gotten round, as you say in English. There you have one of my mottos, one quite appropriate for what I take to be the spirit of the type of 'enlightenment' granted our time. Those who wish to simplify at all costs and who raise a hue and cry about obscurity because they do not recognise the unclarity of the good old *Aufklärung* are in my eyes dangerous dogmatists and tedious obscurantists. No less dangerous (for instance in politics) are those who wish to purify at all costs. (Derrida 1988, p. 119)

'No less dangerous' certainly – somewhat more one would imagine. That is to say, the allusion to (at least) fascism in the context of a complaint about a tendency in philosophy to 'simplify or pretend to be sure of such simplicity where there is none' might seem outrageously hyperbolical. But the point of the comparison is not, I think, without justice. Indeed, by tying a philosophical desire for clarity-through-simplicity to a political desire for (racial, national, ideological, ethnic etc.) purity, Derrida is, I would suggest, re-iterating the basic theme of the passage as a whole; namely, that the question of justice, of doing justice, cannot and so should not be marginalised in considerations concerning philosophy and its inheritances. And there is a *prima facie* case for this, since, as we have seen already, at issue here are countersignatures which, precisely, avow something as 'the *responsible* way of going on'.

This emphasis on questions of justice in this context will be a central feature of the approach to Derrida's treatment of Austin taken in this chapter. An initial and striking indication of the way in which this approach will cut across Williams' characterisation of the current division is that the same issue is also to the fore in *Austin's* reflections on philosophy and the inheritance of philosophy. It will prove helpful to examine this, for the way of going on commended to us by Austin is typically received only in terms of the judicious warning that 'it is not enough to show how clever we are by showing how obscure everything is' (Austin 1979, p. 189).

Austin's most explicit comments on the topic of the inheritance of philosophy appear in the introduction to *Sense and Sensibilia* where he suggests that a satisfactory account of the phenomenon of perception requires that 'here as elsewhere' we 'abandon old habits of *Gleichschaltung*, the deeply ingrained worship of tidy-looking dichotomies' (Austin 1962, p. 3). '*Gleichschaltung*', meaning to bring something into line, to make something conform to a certain standard by force, represents, in its most general aspect, the kind of difficulty Austin identifies in the works of philosophy he criticises, and which he sought to overcome. And as we shall see this is nothing other than an overcoming of the tendency to 'simplify or pretend to be sure of such simplicity where there is none'. Given this kinship to Derrida's remark, it is worth noting that 'Gleichschaltung' has had, since the 1930's, an irreducibly political connotation and that, like 'Führer', is now rarely used. Metaphorised by Hitler, 'Gleichschaltung' was the watchword for the (forced) integration of various previously more or less autonomous bodies (e.g. trade unions, the police, the civil service, the media, the universities) under the control of the National Socialist Party. The word was subsequently appropriated and its meaning further displaced by anti-Nazi's to refer to those who became intellectually integrated into the Party, particularly the intellectual elite (such as Heidegger). 'Gleichschaltung' has, and certainly had at the time Austin was writing, strong overtones of a mind-set which, in the name of purity, forges order by force. Austin's deployment of this word in a philosophical context serves, as it were, as a monogram of his conviction that certain ways of going on are a species of shackled and shackling thinking. In virtue of presenting accounts which are 'too simple' clarity is foregone (ibid., p. 4).

Significantly, when the question of the effect of these habits is broached by Austin we meet again the issue of style. In Austin's view, Gleichschaltung produces a novel kind of linguistic community; a community in which membership is obtained by becoming 'fully masters of a certain special happy style of blinkering philosophical English' (ibid., p. 4). The idea is that a thinker's (typically 'insensible') engagement with time-hallowed ways of formulating and expounding philosophical problems results in the recitation of philosophically familiar line and verse as if its adequacy and pertinence were obvious to everyone. According to Austin, such habits of Gleichschaltung blinker us from the rich understanding of phenomena which we already possess, and so that we cannot see that we are in its sway – although, he stresses, we nevertheless 'feel it to be somehow spurious' (ibid., p. 3).

It is, I think, a major shortcoming of Austin's work that he does not really explore why we find such distorting routines so compelling. Nevertheless, he is sufficiently impressed by their ubiquity to characterise the happy style as intrinsic to philosophy as such:

My general opinion about this doctrine [viz., that we never directly perceive material objects] is that it is a typically scholastic view, attributable, first, to an obsession with a few particular words . . .; and second, to an obsession with a few (and nearly always the same) half-studied 'facts'. I say 'scholastic', but I might just as well have said 'philosophical'; over-simplification, schematisation, and constant obsessive repetition of the same small range of jejune 'examples' are not only peculiar to this case, but far too common to be dismissed as an occasional weakness of philosophers. (*ibid.*, p. 3)

The point is made again in the final paragraph of 'Performative Utterances':

Life and truth and things do tend to be complicated. It's not things, it's philosophers that are simple. You will have heard it said, I expect, that oversimplification is the occupational disease of philosophers, and in one way one might agree with that. But for a sneaking suspicion that it's their occupation. (Austin 1979, p. 252)

It should be obvious that Austin's aversion to clarity-through-simplicity is of a different order to Williams' reservations about the plain style. For Austin, and I will argue for Derrida too, recourse to certain 'tidy-looking dichotomies' does not just threaten injustices in philosophy; rather, it is the distorting idealisation of our language that *is* 'philosophy'. The philosopher is, on this view, one who is happily at home with a way of going on which cannot but fail to do justice to the phenomena. And, naturally enough, in the effort to 'dismantle' its procedures and so, as Austin sees it, 'leave us, in a sense, just where we began' things are bound to be complicated (*ibid.*, p. 5). This is neither complicating 'for the pleasure of complicating' nor does it aim 'to show how clever we are'.

The theme of inheritance is thus itself a more or less constant preoccupation in the writings of Austin and Derrida. Indeed, both seem to write with or out of the desire not to be an heir, or not simply an heir, of philosophy as he found it. Their engagements with philosophy are a kind of disengagement; as it were, a philosophical disinheritance of 'philosophy'. So Derrida infamously aims to 'deconstruct' the classical texts he reads, and Austin for his part aims at what he calls the 'dismantling' of traditional routes of response; the 'abandonment' of philosophy's 'deeply ingrained worship of tidy-looking dichotomies' (Austin 1962, p. 3). Even the terms and topics of their criticism are novel. For example, Derrida charges traditional approaches to language with (among other things) an unjustified subordination or exclusion of writing. And what Austin most insistently hunts down is not a new kind of nonsense (although he finds plenty of that as well) but rather a certain blindness within its familiar procedures: a blindness to aspects of the functioning of language that we, as language users, in fact already grasp.

Whatever the similarity of these gestures of 'deconstruction' and 'dismantling' – and they are considerable – it is with Austin's distinctive appeal to 'the ordinary' that Derrida's criticism of Austin engages most directly. For, according to Derrida, Austin's conception of the ordinary functioning of language remains in the (insensible) grip of inherited presuppositions which can only sustain philosophy's blindness. And to double the irony, Derrida suggests that these are *also* 'the most central presuppositions of the *continental* metaphysical tradition' (Derrida 1988, p. 38).

Insofar as this suggestion acknowledges the presence of the contemporary conviction of a division between analytical and continental philosophy, it does so only to relocate it. The implication would be that when acts of inheritance of 'philosophy' are most active and decisive what really shows itself is the division's non-pertinence. Indeed, Derrida goes so far as to suggest that 'what these "fronts" represent, what weighs upon them both,.. are forces of a *non-philosophical* nature' (*ibid.*). I believe that there is considerable truth to that suggestion, but I will not discuss it here.[6] In what follows I shall be fully occupied with the attempt to present an alternative conception of the terrain, a conception which does justice to the details of the dispute between Austin and Derrida. As I have indicated, I do not think this will point towards a rift between the plain and the obscure, but, as I want to put it, different ways of styling the plain.

II

In 1961 the notes from one of Austin's lecture courses were posthumously published under the title *How to do Things with Words*. These notes made available to a wider audience a style or 'fashion' (Austin 1979, p. 175) of thinking which prior to this had been developed and disseminated almost exclusively in Oxford

---

[6] I have done so at length in 'What is Continental Philosophy?' (Glendinning 1999)

and which indeed became known in the post-war years as 'Oxford Philosophy'.

Despite its nominal independence from Austin, what was called 'Oxford philosophy' didn't really survive Austin's death, at least not as such and not necessarily in Oxford. Nevertheless, many of Austin's students and readers – including an American graduate student working in Oxford called John Searle – remained deeply indebted to their teacher, taking his thoughts abroad and, in time, into such diverse subjects as linguistics, anthropology, literary criticism, and jurisprudence. Austin remains for many an exemplary thinker and critic of traditional philosophy.

Ten years after the publication of *How to do Things with Words*, Jacques Derrida presented a paper called (in English) 'Signature Event Context' (usually abbreviated, dryly, as '*Sec*') to a conference on the theme of communication. Although gaining a reputation as a radical critic of the philosophical tradition, Derrida was suspected by many to be little more that a troublesome obscurantist. That *Sec* seemed to call into question the very possibility of communication as a means of transport of a meaning must have fuelled that suspicion where it failed to provoke meditation.

About a third of *Sec* is devoted to Austin's *How to do Things with Words*. In common with Austin's other writings this text seeks to disrupt the smooth flowing of 'philosophy' by 'dismantling' its insensible habits of *Gleichschaltung*; in this case, by targeting 'the assumption that the business of a "statement" can only be to "describe" some state of affairs, or to "state some fact", which it must do either truly or falsely' (Austin 1980, p. 1). We must, he states, question 'the age-old assumption in philosophy . . . that to say something, at least in all cases worth considering, i.e. all cases considered, is always and simply to state something. This assumption is no doubt unconscious, no doubt precipitate, but it is wholly natural in philosophy apparently' (*ibid.*, p. 12). In the context of Derrida's own critical investigation of a conception of communication as the transference of a meaning-content dominated by an orientation towards truth it is not, therefore, surprising that he should show interest in and admiration for Austin's approach.

On the strength of this interest one could perhaps have hoped for a highly productive confluence of thinking between readers of Austin and readers of Derrida. Unfortunately, however, it has since become the centre of a bitter and sometimes public scene of dispute. And it is in scenes such as this that the idea of a division between analytical and continental traditions has been at its most active. Which is to say that its pertinence to the texts being read did not wait for their reading. Why or when or through whom the idea of this division became the *topos* and title of differences in contemporary philosophy is less important than this: that in the case of Austin and Derrida it has hidden a division which essentially *exceeds* it.

The claim is then that 'it would be a mistake to regard Derrida's discussion of Austin as a confrontation between two prominent philosophical traditions'. This statement is by, of all people, John Searle. In fact, it is the opening sentence of his famously hostile essay 'Reply to Derrida: Reiterating the Differences' (Searle 1977). When Derrida replied in his turn he called this sentence 'the only sentence of the "Reply" to which I can subscribe' (Derrida 1988, p. 37). But Derrida's gesture is hardly consensual. Derrida rejects the hypothesis of confrontation not only because he is suspicious of general appeals to the idea of philosophical division, but also because he considers his own work to be importantly similar to Austin's. Searle's rejection of the hypothesis of confrontation rests, however, on a quite different ground. In Searle's view there *should* have been a confrontation, but because Derrida has so badly 'misunderstood and misstated Austin's position . . . the confrontation never quite takes place' (Searle 1977, p. 198). According to Searle, Derrida took aim but, because his aim was so fundamentally appalling to start with, he missed and the whole thing misfired. It was this mode of reply, the attempt to initiate a confrontation, that drew Derrida's rejoinder, the mammoth essay 'Limited Inc abc . . . ' But the storm did not abate.

I do not intend to restore a perfect order so that the communicative confrontation of traditions can finally take place. And the reason for this is very straightforward, even if it has tended to go unnoticed; namely, that the names 'Austin' and 'Derrida' simply do not represent two prominent philosophical traditions engaged (at last) in a warring conversation. It is more complicated and far more interesting than that. As I have indicated, Derrida says as much himself:

> Among the many reasons that make me unqualified to represent a 'prominent philosophical tradition', there is this one: I consider myself to be in many respects quite close to Austin, both interested in and indebted to his problematic. This is said in *Sec*, very clearly. (Derrida, 1988, p, 38)

Finally then, our question must be: what, after all, has Derrida done with Austin's words on doing things with words?

III

The background to Derrida's engagement with Austin is his (Derrida's) attempt to undermine a conception of 'the meaning' of words and utterances which construes it as something which must be, at least for the speaking subject, 'specific, univocal, and rigorously controllable' (Derrida 1988, p. 1) – an idea which he sometimes presents as the thought that all words are basically names.[7] On this conception, what I *mean* must always be something quite specific, there is, as it were, some definite 'thing' that I, now, mean. Now, according to Derrida, the idea that the meaning of a word or utterance should, ideally, be exact or definite in this way is not one prejudice or injustice among others in philosophy; rather is it *the* philosophical prejudice, *the* philosophical injustice. In the following passage, where Aristotle's account of language is being examined, Derrida makes the general claim quite explicitly: 'A noun is proper when it has but a single sense. Better, it is only in this case that it is properly a noun. Univocity is the essence, or better, the *telos* of language. No philosophy, as such, has ever renounced this Aristotelian ideal. *This ideal is philosophy.*' (Derrida, 1982, p. 247). This distinctively 'philosophical' conception of the essence of language is Derrida's basic target. And, like Austin's condemnation of habits of *Gleichschaltung,* this target is styled not as this or that species of philosophy but as intrinsic to 'philosophy' as such. In posing a radical challenge to this conception it will thus be fundamental to Derrida's mode of being-an-heir to 'philosophy' that even if it is more or less constantly (as he put it at the conference in Reading) '*about* philosophy,…it is not simply "philosophical" through and through'.[8]

In *Sec* there are two central developments of the philosophical conception which are the focus of attention. The first is the idea

---

[7] Making another significant connection, it is notable that Derrida also locates this conception as a central target of Austin's criticism. In a discussion in which he refers to 'things I like in Austin's text ['The Meaning of a Word']', Derrida gives special attention to Austin's singling out 'the curious belief that all words are names, i.e. in effect proper names' (cited by Derrida in 1986, p. 116). Immediately following this quotation Derrida comments that 'this is a gesture essential to deconstruction, it was perhaps its primary gesture: to wonder at that "curious belief"' (*ibid.*).

[8] The full implications of this idea are nicely developed in Darren Sheppard's contribution to this volume.

that an utterance can have 'meaning' only where it possesses a *truth-evaluable* content; the second, is that this content should be essentially *invariant* in different contexts. I will begin with the latter. Against the second of these assumptions Derrida defends what is best seen as a particularly radical form of contextualism.[9] That is, he affirms that there are, in principle, an endless number of different yet non-deviant readings or uses of any 'given' expression. To take an example of the kind used by Charles Travis[10], the utterance 'There's a lot of coffee on the table' can find a use in, and will have a different content in, such cases as where (a) there is a large quantity of brewed coffee on a table; (b) there are a number of sacks of coffee beans on a table; (c) there is a lot of spilt coffee on a table; and so on. Now, these alternatives seem to introduce a shift from a perhaps rather 'ambiguous' utterance formulation to essentially 'unambiguous' situations. However, according to Derrida's contextualism, each of the alternatives would, *as utterances*, be just as open to an endless number of non-deviant readings as the first. Of course, if a reader of the original sentence took the utterance as an assertion of the type (a) when, as one will say, the speaker 'meant' (b), the misunderstanding *could* be removed by supplying the formulation in (b). But there is no point at which one reaches a formulation which would simply fix the sense *unambiguously*.

This point runs extremely deeply. For, as I have indicated, a defender of the philosophical conception is likely to think that, at least for the speaking subject, there is some specific thing that is (perhaps on some 'specific context' of a speaking of it) *the* 'meaning' of the utterance. This is the idea of there being what Derrida calls an 'intentional meaning' which allows for 'no dissemination escaping the horizon of the unity of meaning' (Derrida 1988, p. 14): a 'meaning' with respect to which the room for alternative non-deviant readings has, as it were, been completely removed. Here, it is supposed, what I (now) mean or intend by my utterance is completely *sharp*. But according to Derrida, it is a logical

---

[9] Although Derrida will insist that words and signs must have an identity which is independent of any particular context (that is, we must be able to recognise 'the same' sign in different contexts), the idea that I am picking up on here is his claim that 'there are only contexts without any center or absolute anchorage' (Derrida 1988, p. 12). I have provided only a sketch of Derrida's account in what follows. A more comprehensive discussion of Derrida's argument can be found in Glendinning 2000, pp. 274–283.

[10] C. Travis 1989, pp. 18–19.

incoherence to suppose that there could be marks or signs (inner or outer) which might have this property. We cannot, he argues, make sense of some 'event' being, say, an utterance, if the possibility of other such 'events' ('events' in which *other* possibilities of 'communicating something' with it 'take place') are not included in our description of it. That is, for Derrida, openness to such possibilities is part of the structure of the event, not merely something which might, now and then, come to pass. So Derrida is not simply advancing a claim about the (factual) repeatability or multiple applicability of words and signs in different contexts, but a claim about the 'eventhood' of such events; namely, that the possibility of such 'other' repetitions is internal to its *being* that kind of event. And this holds for any specification or individuation of 'what', on some occasion, is 'meant' by an utterance. That is, the functioning of an utterance on this occasion (the possibility of 'meaning something' or 'communicating something' 'here and now') is inseparable from, what Derrida calls its 'iterability'; a quasi-technical term he uses to capture this 'logic that ties repetition to alterity' (*ibid.*, p.7).

It is part of this conception that any attempt to restrict 'acceptable' instances to contexts 'determined by an epistemic intention' or 'within a horizon of truth' (*ibid.*, p. 12), that is, to contexts in which there is a specifically truth-evaluable content, is also unacceptably dogmatic. There is no reason, no logical reason, which would prohibit us from affirming the possibility of the iteration of signs or expressions in ways which are not truth-evaluable and yet which do not lose all possibility of functioning. It is at this point that the criticism of the second traditional assumption, the assumption of the invariance of meaning (communication as that which 'circulates a representation' which would be indefinitely repeatable as 'the same' in every context of its use (*ibid.*, p. 6)), meets the first traditional assumption, where communication is 'limited strictly to the transference of a semantic content that is already constituted and dominated by an orientation toward truth' (*ibid.*, pp. 13–4). It is obviously also where Derrida's discussion meets up with and is close to Austin's analysis of the performative. Indeed, with this conclusion, we can see very clearly why Derrida declared a special interest in (and admiration for) Austin's ideas. However, in the next section I will examine Derrida's claim that, despite its promise to 'shatter' the traditional conception of 'meaning' (*ibid.*, p. 13), Austin's analysis 'has not taken into account in the structure of locution' the essential iterability of every event of language (*ibid.*, p. 14). As I have indicated, if Derrida's reading is correct then Austin's analysis remains blinkered by just the kind of habit of *Gleichschaltung* which, elsewhere, he aims to dismantle.

IV

Anyone familiar with Austin's analyses of the intricacies and irreducible complexities of the use of language will readily see why Derrida is interested in them. But Derrida's treatment of Austin's work is not wholly uncritical. Specifically, he argues that as a consequence of a dogmatic affirmation of 'a tidy-looking dichotomy' Austin's procedures are unable to take full account of the acknowledged 'ritual or ceremonial' character (Austin, 1980, p. 19) of 'locutionary acts' (acts to be described as 'saying certain words'). It will bear stressing that this affirmation is inseparable from a countersignature of a quite specific way of going on. For, it is with this affirmation that Austin's analysis is forced into *non-logical* exclusions of possibilities of the phenomenon of language – what Austin calls 'marginal' and 'parasitic' cases – which will return us to the question of the inheritance of 'philosophy'.

It has been noted that the target of Austin's argumentation in *How to do Things with Words* is 'the assumption that the business of a "statement" can only be to "describe" some state of affairs, or to "state some fact", which it must do either truly or falsely' (*ibid.*, p. 1). Austin's criticism of this conception is developed through the identification and examination of what he calls 'performative utterances'. By essential contrast to (true/false) 'constative utterances', the functioning of the performative is not to be conceived in terms of the communication of a meaning-content that is oriented towards an assessment in terms of truth (*ibid.*, p. 12). The performative does not describe or represent something that exists outside the speech-act, rather it is a public performance that *does* something by making use of, by conforming to, a conventional procedure. For example,

the utterance 'I do' (take this woman to be my lawful wedded wife), as uttered in the course of a marriage ceremony. Here we should say that in saying these words we are *doing* something – namely, marrying, rather than *reporting* something, namely *that* we are marrying. And the act of marrying, like, say, the act of betting, is at least *preferably* (though still not *accurately*) to be described as *saying certain words*, rather than as performing a different, inward and spiritual, action of which these words are merely the outward and audible sign. (*ibid.*, pp. 12–3)

So, with the emphasis on public uses of words, it would appear that Austin has succeeded in avoiding, not only the idea that the 'meaning' of an utterance must be a truth-evaluable content, but also the idea that there must be some specific 'intentional content' which fixes the sense unambiguously. According to Derrida, however, he has not. For in Derrida's view, certain fundamental and ineliminable features of Austin's analysis guarantees that the promise of performative communication is not fulfilled. The details of Austin's analysis have the consequence that, 'performative communication becomes once more the communication of an intentional meaning, even if that meaning has no referent in the form of a thing or a prior or exterior state of things' (Derrida 1988, p. 14). And, as we shall see, by an 'intentional meaning' Derrida is attributing to Austin a conception which precisely allows 'no dissemination escaping the horizon of the unity of meaning' (*ibid.*). In what follows, and partly independently of Derrida's argument, I will trace a route to this conclusion.

While Austin's analysis of the performative focuses on what we do with words, he does not think that the performative can be fully or fully accurately described simply as an act of saying certain words. Part of what Austin is suggesting here is that, in general, 'if the act is to be deemed to have been performed . . . the circumstances, including other actions, must be appropriate' (Austin 1980, p. 9). Now, it is a fundamental feature of Austin's view that the intention of the speaker is included among the requisites here. On its own that is, of course, no objection at all, and Derrida too wishes to retain the category of intention within any satisfactory account of 'forms of iteration' with signs (Derrida 1988, p. 18). However, what would be problematic, according to Derrida, is if the treatment of this category took no account of the iterability which must structure every intention, just as much as any (intended or unintended) locution. And this is indeed Derrida's complaint: the Austinian analysis will require the 'conscious and intentional presence' of the speaker 'in the totality of the operation' (*ibid.*, p. 14), an intentional presence which, on an occasion of utterance, serves to isolate and fix the content unambiguously. As we have seen, Derrida considers such attempts to fix content in this way as betraying a non-logical moment of any analysis. As I see it, it is at this point that the issue of the inheritance of 'philosophy' becomes decisive. That is, Austin's procedures cannot be fully grasped independently of a crucial 'countersignature' of a specific way of going on. Indeed, in my view it involves an unquestioned endorsement of a distinctively Fregean conception of the analysis of the '*force*' of an utterance. This is not something in view in Derrida's reading of Austin,[11] but it will prove useful to examine this in some detail.

In 'The Thought' Frege introduces the notion of force in the context of an analysis of the logic and limits of communication. Sentences with force are those which communicate thoughts. Now, because Frege's defines a thought as 'something for which the question of truth arises' (Frege 1967, p. 20), he (basically) restricts the notion of force to sentences in which we 'state something' (*ibid.*, p. 21).[12] This is, of course, precisely the restriction that Austin aims to lift in his analysis of performative communication, and it is almost fortuitous that Frege is willing to admit to the class of sentences with a force anything except indicative sentences. However, the important point is that the concept of force is introduced by Frege not because there are, besides indicative sentences, sentences that express the same thought in another way. Rather, as we shall see, it is introduced in order to distinguish genuine from merely apparent cases of the communication of thoughts, *however* the thought is conveyed.

Frege holds that sentential realisation cannot of itself guarantee that an event of speech is a genuine case of a communication of a thought. An indicative sentence-token may lack what he calls

[11] In fact, Derrida takes the introduction of 'the value of force' to be 'moving in the direction of Nietzsche' (p. 13). I do not want to simply dismiss that proposal, but I do want to insist that the Fregean connection is both more direct and more decisive.

[12] Frege famously includes interrogatives among the class of sentences which can communicate something. With sentence-questions, he states, 'we expect to hear "yes" or "no". The answer "yes" means the same as an indicative sentence, for in it the thought that was already completely contained in the interrogative sentence is laid down as true' (Frege 1967, p. 21). Again, the important point with respect to the notion of force is that for Frege it applies only to events of speech in which thoughts are laid down as true. That is, it does not seem to be intended to highlight a component of sentences which is variable between sentences that can express the same thought. As the quotation indicates, strictly speaking it is the answer 'yes' and not the interrogative sentence itself that can possess force.

'real assertive force' because, according to Frege, we do not actually have a case of communication unless the thought it expresses is, on some occasion, 'actually being put forward as true' (*ibid.*, p. 22). For this reason Frege has to accept that any sentence-type that can be uttered with real assertive force can also be uttered without it:

> This happens when we do not speak seriously. As stage thunder is only apparent thunder and a stage fight is only an apparent fight, so stage assertion is only apparent assertion. It is only acting, only fancy. In his part the actor asserts nothing, nor does he lie, even if he says something of whose falsehood he is convinced. In poetry we have the case of thoughts being expressed without actually being put forward as true in spite of the form of the indicative sentence. Therefore it must still always be asked, about what is presented in the form of an indicative sentence, whether it really contains an assertion. And this question must be answered in the negative if the requisite seriousness is lacking. (*ibid.*, p. 22.)

Any sentence-type is, as it were, the standing possibility for tokens that either do or do not possess real assertive force; and whether sentence-tokens do or not is a matter of whether the circumstances were ones in which the use of words was or was not an expression of a thought 'being put forward as true'.

Returning now to Austin, it is, I believe, of enormous significance that an anonymous objection which he poses to his idea that the performative is 'to be described as *saying certain words*' is clearly Fregean:

> [It is true that] if the act is to be deemed to have been performed . . . the circumstances, including other actions, must be appropriate. But we may, in objecting, have something totally different, and this time quite mistaken, in mind . . . Surely the words must be spoken 'seriously' and so as to be taken 'seriously'? (Austin 1980, pp. 8–9)

As we have seen, Austin's official position is explicitly opposed to the idea that performative utterances are merely the outward sign of 'inward and spiritual' actions. However, his response to this 'quite mistaken' objection is complicated:

> Surely the words must be spoken 'seriously' and so as to be taken 'seriously'? This is, though vague, true enough in general

– an important commonplace in discussing the purport of any utterance whatsoever. I must not be joking, for example, nor writing a poem. But we are apt to have a feeling that their being serious consists in their being uttered as merely the outward and visible sign, for convenience or other record or for information, of an inward and spiritual act. (*ibid.*, p. 9)

Austin's endorsing, if qualified, countersignature of a way of going on is transparent. With respect to his qualification, however, it is crucial to see that it cannot be interpreted as a rejection of Frege's account. It is true that for Frege if the thought expressed by the indicative sentence *was* laid down as true then that is so in virtue of the fact that a speaker must, at the time, have intended to do just that. But this does not mean that the utterance-event is, for Frege, merely 'a description, true or false, of the occurrence of [an] inward performance'. On the contrary, for Frege, when and if the thought expressed is laid down as true 'the real assertive force lies . . . in the form of the indicative sentence' (Frege 1967, p. 22). And my claim will be that, notwithstanding Austin's official position, far from rejecting the Fregean requirement that a distinctive 'inward' act take place in serious speech, Austin's analysis, on all essentials, confirms it. In what follows I will explain this.

For Frege, the basic way in which a (genuine) assertion can 'go wrong' is by the thoughts expressed being false. But this kind of occasion still resides within the space of communication because it still concerns an event in which expressed thoughts are being put forward as true. What takes us outside the space of genuine 'communication' for Frege are occasions in which thoughts are merely expressed; that is, expressed without being put forward as true. That Austin retains the general shape of this Fregean picture can be seen by attending to his methodological programme of isolating what he calls 'the happy performative' (Austin 1980, p. 12f).

Like Frege, Austin develops his analysis by focusing on ways in which occasions of the use of words 'can be and go wrong' (*ibid.*, p. 14). In the case of performative communication, however, the basic fault cannot be that the utterance is false. But Austin's analysis contains a structural analogue. As Cavell notes, 'Austin "substitutes" for the logically defined concept of truth . . . [the concept of] "felicity"' (Cavell 1994, p. 81). And so, as Austin puts it, 'we call the doctrine of the things that can be and go wrong on the occasion of such utterances, the doctrine of the *Infelicities*' (Austin

1980, p. 14).[13] Such infelicities parallel Frege's treatment of stating falsehoods in that they are included within the space of performative communication. And, for identical reasons: such cases are still events of speech in which, *in a special way,* 'saying certain words' (Frege's 'expressing thoughts') is not all there is to it. We can begin to clarify what more Austin requires by exploring the passages in which he excludes two possibilities of the use of performative utterances from his (current) considerations; possibilities which relate to what he conceives of as non-standard or abnormal cases. Such cases are ones in which we would say either that the performance of the act was not 'done' at all (the possibility that the speech-*act* was not performed *freely* – first exclusion) or that the words of the speech-act were uttered in a way which is 'parasitic upon its normal use' (the possibility that the words were used not *seriously* – second exclusion).

The possibility specifically related to speech-acts as utterances (the second 'Fregean' exclusion) is our primary concern. Still sticking closely to the Fregean analysis, it involves the possibility for any utterance (performative or otherwise) to be used in stage recitation or fiction. In the case of performatives this involves situations in which the speaker is not putting forward what is said with the intention actually to perform the speech-act whose formula is being uttered. Austin insists that this possibility is a special kind of 'ill' which can befall the utterance:

> As *utterances* our performatives are *also* heir to certain other kinds of ill which infect *all* utterances. And these likewise . . . **we are deliberately at present excluding.** I mean, for example, the following: a performative utterance will, for example, be *in a peculiar way* **hollow or void** if said by an actor on the stage, or if introduced in a poem, or spoken in soliloquy . . . Language in such circumstances is in special way – intelligibly – used not **seriously,** but in ways *parasitic* upon its normal use... **All this we are excluding from consideration.** Our performative utterances, felicitous or not, are to be **understood as issued in ordinary circumstances.** (*ibid.,* pp. 21–22. Austin's italics, my bold.)

---

[13] Since the conditions of felicity that Austin (actually) considers are essentially conventional, it is at best misleading of Cavell to say that infelicitousness is a matter of failing to be 'adequate to reality' (Cavell 1994, p. 81). However, he is right to criticize Derrida for supposing that, for truth, Austin 'at times' substitutes 'the value of force' (Derrida 1988, p. 13). This being admitted, we must not overlook the fact that if (like Austin) we aim to lift the Fregean restriction, what the *special* infelicities (those which Austin 'excludes from current consideration') affect would be, precisely, the force of the utterance.

Austin aims to exclude from his consideration of performative communication just those occasions in which what he wants to call the 'ordinary circumstances' of speech are not in place. And with this in view it seems undeniable that, for good or ill, Austin's concept of the ordinary is, as Derrida puts it, 'marked' by this exclusion (Derrida 1988, p. 16). For good or ill? That is the question. That Austin's analysis involves an endorsing 'countersignature' of a certain way of going on is clear. But does this show that Derrida is right to see this way of going on as betraying a 'metaphysical decision' (*ibid.*, p. 93)? Or is it rather that Derrida's affirmation of dissemination leads to the absurd denial of the possibility of distinguishing between serious and non-serious utterances? Has Austin, in accepting the 'important commonplace', really committed himself to 'a strategy fraught with metaphysical presupposition' (*ibid.*, p. 85)?

In Austin's defence both Searle and (from a completely different angle) Cavell have insisted that the moments of exclusion which Derrida highlights are merely strategic or methodological deferrals not motivated attempts to define a context of the 'ordinary circumstances' of communication oriented towards a 'metaphysical' ideal. Thus Cavell insists that the exclusions in *How to do Things with Words* are simply exclusions *from that work*, and moreover, ones which are taken up directly (if not entirely happily) in the papers published as 'A Plea for Excuses' and 'Pretending'. As he puts it, 'what the doctrine of excuses does for cases of extenuation, Austin's work represented in his paper "Pretending" in part does for, and is meant eventually to do more for, cases of etiolation, parasitism, and in general the realm of the "non-serious"' (Cavell 1994, p. 91). In short, just as Searle had classed the exclusions as 'a matter of research strategy' (Searle 1977, p. 205), so Cavell sees them as a matter of 'contingent convenience' (Cavell 1995, p. 71). This kind of claim takes us to the heart of the Austin/Derrida debate. In what follows I aim to show why the Searle/Cavell response is inadequate.

V

It is clear, I think, that Austin is committed to a kind of 'ideal' speech situation in the sense that the terms of his analysis of infelicities as 'what can go wrong' at least introduces the possibility of an ideal case or situation in which, as it were, *'everything* goes right'. From this perspective, the *possibility* which Austin acknowledges as one to which *all* speech acts, as such, are necessarily heir is represented only as an *eventuality*, and of a type which strays too far from the ideal circumstances to count as 'ordinary'; *qua* eventuality this type constitutes a different order of infelicity, 'a sea-change in special circumstances' (Austin 1980, p. 22). Derrida's objection is that Austin, blinkered by the 'important commonplace', is insufficiently sensitive to the necessity he has acknowledged. Instead of pursuing an investigation of the structure of locutionary acts which shows why this 'risk', *qua possibility*, is essential to its *being* such an act, his procedure passes over the general logic of locutions and positions it, *qua eventuality*, as something that transgresses the 'ordinary circumstances' of language use – something that can, and therefore should, be pared away or excluded from an analysis of the 'normal use' of words in 'ordinary circumstances'.

The central issue between Austin and Derrida can thus be posed with the question whether this paring away is, even in principle, an ambition which might succeed. Searle and Cavell clearly assume that it can; consideration of 'the realm of the "non-serious"' can be put off until later. Derrida, on the other hand, is equally convinced that it cannot. Have we here finally reached the place of confrontation of two traditions? Unless analytical philosophy is to be characterised by a lack of concern for the structure of 'ordinary language' this cannot be so. For the reason why Derrida is convinced that consideration of 'the realm of the "non-serious"' cannot be put off until later can only be understood in terms of such a concern. Specifically, his claim is that because it is internal to the structure of 'the realm of the "serious"' (the realm which Austin's analysis aims, *here and now*, to consider) that it possesses features held by Austin to define the excluded realm, then in this case, and *pace* Searle and Cavell, 'you cannot root-out the "parasite" without rooting-out the "standard" at the same time' (*ibid.*, p. 90). I will explain this.

One way of putting Derrida's claim is to say that there is a structural or internal relation between the two realms. Derrida attempts to make this relation perspicuous by describing *non*-citational utterances as being, essentially, 'the modification of a general citationality' (Derrida 1988, p. 18). This is not to be taken to imply that non-citational utterances cannot be contrasted with, say, events of speech on stage in a theatre. Rather the point is that this contrast can arise (can be *constructed*) only within a 'general space of possibility' which is characterised by the citational in the sense that iterability is essential to *all* locutionary acts. Thus, as iterable units, non-citational utterances do not 'emerge *in opposition to* citationality' since the everyday distinction cannot appear *as such* outside a space of 'a general citationality or iterability' (*ibid.*).

So in Derrida's view the type of eventuality that Austin deems 'outside' the scope of the ordinary is, *qua* possibility, part of the essential structure of every event capable of communicating whatsoever. Again it must be emphasised that Derrida's view does *not* imply that 'ordinary language' is not serious or is really fictional. But it does challenge the idea that 'the realm of the "serious"' can be defined in terms of the presence at the time of speaking of a conscious mental state (supposedly an intention) which escapes the logic of iterability. Indeed, for Derrida 'part of the most originary essence of ["non-fiction-standard discourse"] is to allow fiction, the simulacrum, parasitism, to take place – and in so doing to "de-essentialize" itself as it were' (Derrida 1988, p. 133).

On this view, as long as one's concern is with the logic of ordinary language the 'realm of the "non-serious"' cannot even provisionally be excluded. But what if, with Austin, one supposed otherwise? It should be clear that to do so would require that what will distinguish 'the realm of the "serious"' (namely, and *ex hypothesi*, the presence of a speaker's *vouloir dire*) is something which is capable of specification or individuation in terms which are restricted to what, on any occasion, is actually *present* in the circumstances of such speech. In order to see how problematic this assumption is we should remember that the addition of further 'outward' *words* (such as 'I intend this seriously') cannot be assumed to settle the question; for they too can be used without the requisite seriousness. So, what is specified as present here will have to be construed as something whose intrinsic character would determine the seriousness of the utterance. But given the constraints imposed by the exclusion, what can be identified by this analysis will perforce stand as something potentially unique: it would make sense to say that *it* took place or occurred without importing into one's description of *it* any essential reference to 'other' such events. Thus, what we will specify is something which *could* occur only once; for, and again given the restrictions imposed by the exclusion, other iterations can be construed *only* as a possible occurrence and not as essential to its being the kind of process or act we wish to specify. But the question whether we can attribute meaning to *anything* specified in this way – that is, independently of 'the iteration structuring it' (*ibid.*, p. 18) – is a logical and not a psychological one. To put this in terms familiar from Wittgenstein's writing, the question is whether what (given the constraint) is supposed to be the specification or individuation of an intention to perform a certain speech-act can possibly *be* such? Anything (and so nothing) will count as 'speaking in accordance' with what we manage to specify. Such, according to Derrida, is the inevitable consequence of Austin's procedures when it accepts the 'commonplace' distinction – that tidy-looking habit of *Gleichschaltung* – between serious and non-serious utterances in his analysis of the performative.

This argument suggests that Austin's procedure of excluding 'the realm of the "non-serious"'' is not 'merely strategic' but profoundly oriented towards a quite specific metaphysics of locutionary acts. And it is this that Derrida aims to register with the claim that, in Austin's account, 'performative communication becomes once more the communication of an intentional meaning', a meaning which, in its description, 'implies teleologically…no dissemination escaping the horizon of the unity of meaning'. Of course, if Derrida's argument is right then this 'intentional meaning' is no meaning at all.

What then is really at stake in the relation between Austin and Derrida? Both will want to say that performative utterances made in 'ordinary circumstances' are, *when compared to the ideal*, 'impure' (see Austin 1980, p. 150). However, it should be noted that when Derrida 'adopts the word "impure"' from Austin, he (Derrida) wishes to stress that 'impurity' is an irreducible structural or 'original' feature of *all* locutionary acts, and so it is not conceived, as it is for Austin, as something that just typically comes to pass. (Derrida 1988, p. 17). Austin's appeal to ordinary language promises to escape what he calls 'the snags and lures' of philosophical simplification and schematic idealisation which 'casts the philosopher out of the garden of the world we live in' (Austin 1979, p. 90). What Derrida shows in his reading of Austin is that this appeal remains oriented towards an inherited ideal of the functioning of ('ordinary') language which cannot but maintain our exile.

This is not to say that Derrida has developed an alternative approach to ordinary language that is 'confident of knowing what it is, where it begins and where it ends' (Derrida 1988, p. 89). But this is, of course, of the essence of the ordinary as Derrida thinks it. It is part of the iterable structure of language in general that it is indefinitely open to future contingencies which are *a priori* illimitable by an essential definition – and as such our language '"de-essentializes" itself as it were'. So the logic of iterability cannot justify a new and more rigorous distinction between what is and what is not (from case to case) called 'ordinary' or 'extraordinary' in our use of language. But it does entail a relation to 'philosophy' which is *bound* (duty/necessity) to resist restrictive interpretations of the ordinary. As Derrida put it at the end of the *Ratio* conference, when we are referring to the functioning of 'ordinary language' 'the reference is to something which is simply an open space for transformation. Thus it is on the question of the delimitation of "ordinary language" that the issue of "metaphysics" and "metaphysical origins" arises.' (Derrida, p. 118). For this reason, when what is in question are ways of going on with 'philosophy', the work of thinking finds itself governed by a single or endlessly singular task: to be just, to do justice to 'the ordinary'. And 'the ordinary', not as something to be simply opposed to 'the extraordinary', but (and Derrida acknowledged that 'this is close to the Wittgenstein that [Mulhall] presented' (*ibid.*)) as a space which is essentially 'vulnerable' to or not 'immune' to the extraordinary. And that also means: essentially vulnerable to the desire for finding simplicity or purity or exactness where there is none.

The case of Austin and Derrida will never have been a contrast or contest between analytical and continental philosophy. Indeed, conceiving it as a confrontation between two traditions of this kind is wholly inappropriate and superficial. Both thinkers aim to do justice to the possibilities of the phenomenon of language. Perhaps the lesson of Derrida's reading of Austin is just how difficult it is to avoid a preconceived ideal of its structure and functioning to which we think reality *must*, in some way, correspond (cp. Wittgenstein 1968, §131). In my view, it is with respect to this tendency to simplify and idealise the actual structure and functioning of language that works of contemporary philosophy should be judged. And it is here, and not with a dogmatic conviction in the philosophical pertinence of the analytical/continental division, that our mode of inheriting 'philosophy' becomes decisive. Indeed, it becomes possible to see why being-an-heir to 'philosophy' is inseparable from decisions with respect to what one calls the 'ordinary' or 'standard' or 'everyday'.[14]

References

Austin, J.L. (1962). *Sense and Sensibilia.* Oxford: Oxford University Press.
Austin, J.L. (1979). *Philosophical Papers.* Oxford: Oxford University Press.
Austin, J.L. (1980). *How to do Things with Words.* Oxford: Oxford University Press.
Cavell, S. (1979). *The Claim of Reason.* Oxford: Oxford University Press.
Cavell, S. (1994). *A Pitch of Philosophy.* Cambridge, Mass.: Harvard University Press.
Cavell, S. (1995). *Philosophical Passages.* Oxford: Blackwell.
Derrida, J. (1986). *Memoires for Paul de Man.* New York: Columbia University Press.
Derrida, J. (1982). *Margins of Philosophy.* Trans. A. Bass. Brighton: The Harvester Press.
Derrida, J. (1988). *Limited Inc.* Evanston: North Western University Press.
Dummett, M. (1996). Interview with Fabrice Pataut, in *Philosophical Investigations,* 19:1.
Frege, G. (1967). 'The Thought: A Logical Enquiry', in P.F. Strawson (ed.) *Philosophical Logic.* Oxford: Oxford University Press.
Glendinning, S. (1999). 'What is Continental Philosophy?', in S. Glendinning (ed.) *The Edinburgh Encyclopedia of Continental Philosophy.* Edinburgh: Edinburgh University Press.
Glendinning, S. (2000). 'Communication and Writing: A Public Language Argument', *Proceedings of the Aristotelian Society,* Vol. 100.
Searle, J.R. (1977). 'Reiterating the Differences: A Reply to Derrida', *Glyph,* Vol. 1.
Travis, C. (1989). *The Uses of Sense.* Oxford: Clarendon Press.
Williams, B. (1985). *Ethics and the Limits of Philosophy.* Cambridge: Cambridge University Press.
Williams, B. (1996). 'Contemporary Philosophy: A Second Look', in N. Bunnin and E.P. Tsui-James (eds.) *The Blackwell Companion to Philosophy.* Oxford: Oxford University Press.
Wittgenstein, L. (1968). *Philosophical Investigations.* Trans. G.E.M. Anscombe. Oxford: Basil Blackwell.

[14] I would like to thank John Cottingham, Hans-Johann Glock, Colin Radford, Gabriel Segal and Sean Sayers for comments on earlier drafts of this paper. I would also like to record my debt to Stephen Mulhall for many conversations on Austin and Derrida 'in quest of the ordinary' and also to Bernard Williams whose generous (but until now unacknowledged) response to my request for clarification of his views in 1996 helped me to think more clearly about the analytical/continental division. Some of the material in this paper is a development of an approach to Derrida's reading of Austin that can be found in my *On Being With Others: Heidegger-Wittgenstein-Derrida* (London: Routledge, 1998). I am grateful to the publishers for allowing me to make use of that material here.

John Cottingham (chair): Good morning everyone and a warm welcome to the 1999 *Ratio* conference hosted by the Philosophy Department at the University of Reading. We have had many very distinguished philosophical speakers at these conferences but none I think more distinguished than our guest of honour today, who is himself the theme of this conference. We are delighted to welcome Jacques Derrida to Reading.

To start the day's events we have Geoffrey Bennington, Professor of French at the University of Sussex. Geoffrey Bennington is very well known as a translator of Jacques Derrida's work, has collaborated with him on a book and is also a major force in the presentation of Derrida's ideas to the anglophone philosophical and academic community. His paper is called 'For the Sake of Argument (Up to a Point)'.

FOR THE SAKE OF ARGUMENT
(UP TO A POINT)

Geoffrey Bennington

This is, perhaps, not very philosophical. This is theatre. Or even cinema. *C'est du cinéma.* Television. What fun.

I

We are here to act, and to act something out. A play. A scene. Something perhaps not very philosophical, more of the order of drama. Call this scene something like: Derrida (finally) meets the (real) philosophers. You would like to get on with it, wouldn't you, get down to brass tacks, to arguments, to start finally sorting some things out. That is what you came for, I imagine, on the basis of some assumed promise or imagined contract whereby we would dispense with the theatricals for once, do without the messing about, eschew the word-play and fancy talk, and finally get down to thrashing out the real issues, the points, the arguments,

get down to work, to *business*, stop being on holiday, stop the
engine just idling, find out who or what wears the trousers, as I am
told Austin used to say (not very philosophically, perhaps). Good
will on both sides here (assuming there *are* sides, and that there
are *only two* sides if there are sides) depends on our respecting, in
Derrida's presence, the rather minimal contract defined, in the
title of the conference, by the notions of *arguing* or *argument*.
As Simon Glendinning's playful title suggests, this is already
not simple (and therefore, we might assume, in need of further
analysis): we (or you at least, in my more or less fictional or
theatrical – perhaps rather hysterical – construction or imagination of you, because *my* position here is of course ambiguous,
both painful and enjoyable, marginal and pivotal, a sort of
'vanishing mediator' for what Stanley Cavell calls, not very philosophically, I fear, 'the French-German side of the philosophical
mind'[1])– you are here to *argue with* Derrida. And that seems
immediately to suggest at least three possibilities: 1) you are here
to engage in reasonable and reasoned argument or debate with
Jacques Derrida, here present as a party to that argument, who
will have more or less solemnly promised (and we know from
Limited Inc all about his solemn promises) to enter into the spirit
of the thing, to *argue* or to enter into argument, to put up arguments recognisable as such in the codes of what the French often
tend to call *la philosophie anglo-saxonne*, and that here, in Britain at
least, is most often, I think, just called 'philosophy' – and in principle this type of discussion could bear on anything at all; 2) you
are here to argue with Derrida in the sense of entering into
dispute with him, here present, in the sense of putting up arguments *against* him, to contest what he has written and said, to get
into polemical discussion with him (although somewhere he says
that he detests discussion) perhaps even to attack him, to harass
him or give him a hard time (this seems to be the etymologically
primitive sense of the verb argue in Old French[2]), to get into a

---

[1]   Stanley Cavell, *Philosophical Passages* (Oxford: Blackwell, 1995), p. 45. On the following page, Cavell refers more cautiously to 'the, or a, Continental tradition'.
   [2]   Littré's historical entries for the verb give the following, with a clear shift towards the
modern sense after the fourteenth century:
XIe s. Qui de bataille s'arguent et hasteient, Ch. de Rol. LXXVI.
XIIe s. Rolanz senti que la mort mout l'argue, Ronc. p. 104. La nuit, quant s'amour m'argue, Couci, Dame de Faiel. Li altre l'arguent et reprenent et dient k'il soffrir ne puient la
perece de sa tevor [tiédeur] . . . . ST BERN. 567.
XIIIe s. Et tout fussent mort se ne fust la chevalerie . . . . qui soustint le fais des Sarrasins,

row, to score some points at any rate; 3) you are here to argue with Derrida in the sense of *using* Derrida for the purpose of arguing – Derrida (no longer quite so *present* as seems necessary for the first two scenarios, a little more spectral this time, not so directly interpellated as in the first two scenes, more of a spectator) would in this case be a *source* of more or less telling arguments that could be wielded to potentially good purpose in *other* debates, what we might think of as 'domestic' issues perhaps within Anglo-Saxon philosophy, such as the so-called 'problem of other minds' or the 'private-language' question, problems about which Derrida may well not explicitly have written, and with which he may not even be familiar in the terms in which these problems are habitually put within Anglo-Saxon philosophy – indeed he may not even think that these *are* the main problems of philosophy, nor even perhaps that philosophy is essentially about solving problems at all – but to which his thinking might be taken (or used) to contribute, perhaps once it has been sufficiently re-written or transcribed in the form of, precisely, *arguments*. And in this last case Derrida, here present after all, might be content to look on and listen, perhaps a little surprised or perplexed or even amused to find just what he can be used to argue for or against.

II

What is arguing; what is an argument? The word and concept 'argument' has a history, like other concepts, and we inherit something of that history with the concept, which needs *reading* in and against that history. (I believe I am right in saying that 'analytic philosophy' has recently become more interested in questions of philosophical history, especially perhaps its own history.) It is a word and concept with quite a rich history (though

qui moult les arguoient, Chr. de Rains, 93. Coart le lievres moult s'argue De cort en cort, de rue en rue, Ren. 11071. Mes cil mauvesement arguent, la Rose, 6302.

XIVe s. Et ne te dois nul temps meler d'**arguer** ne de contredire chose que tu lui oies dire, BRUYANT dans Ménagier, t. II, p. 22. Et par ceste difference povons nous **arguer** à cest propos, ORESME, Eth. 27. Qui diroit ou **arguer**oit ainsy : la terre est entre le soleil et la lune, ID. ib. 5. Maistres Thumas, dist il, vous parlés folement ; J'**arguer**ai à vous ; car je sai bien comment : Uns mos de l'escripture vous desmontre et aprent, Baud. de Seb. XII, 321.

XVe s. Logique qui enseigne **arguer**, et entre le vray et fauls discerner, CHRIST. DE PISAN, Charles V, III, ch. 11. D'autre costé on le **arguer**oit de sa promesse. COMM. II, 1. Il ne me appartenoit pas de **arguer** ny parler contre son plaisir, ID. V, 13.

XVIe s. Le regime des choses humaines argue si clairement de la providence de Dieu qu'on ne la sauroit nier, CALV. Inst. 22. Ses mouvemens et ses contenances arguent et monstrent grande foiblesse et bassesse, AMYOT, Comment refréner la colère, 14.

perhaps not a very clear-cut *philosophical* history – I imagine that
Aristotle would normally be credited with first formulating a
theory of argument (this is certainly the case in a recent French
philosophical encyclopedia I was able to consult):[3] and in that
case, argument (though the Greek word thus translated (for
example at the beginning of the *Topics* [101b, 13 and 16]) is,
perhaps not surprisingly, *logos*) is already philosophically starting
to fall short in some sense, more on the side of the probable and
the doxical than of the apodeictic or the demonstrable.
Arguments are needed when proofs or demonstrations are lacking, and in Cicero and Quintilian (in both of whom the term
argumentum appears thematically) they are invoked in the service
of mere persuasion, of rhetoric.[4] The concept of 'argument' may
be a philosophical concept, but, like many others, it is not
unequivocally a concept *of philosophy*, belonging to philosophy.
Let us say that argument is only ambiguously philosophical,
perhaps not very philosophical. And beyond the two or three
senses I have exploited so far, an argument can, in a slightly different sense, be 'an outward sign or indication of something'
(Webster gives Shakespeare's, 'it is no addition to her wit nor no
great argument of her folly'; cf. Littré's similar example with the
verb 'arguer', from Calvin, where the outward sign is more clearly
a reason to believe something: 'Le regime des choses humaines
argue si clairement de la providence de Dieu qu'on ne la sauroit
nier', CALV. Inst. 22, or with the noun, this time inciting to
action: 'Dieu nous donne argument continuel de le prier et
louer', CALV. Inst. 707). I can imagine that from the 'Anglo-
Saxon' point of view (but I am certainly simplifying it by calling it
'a' point of view) an argument in this sense – perhaps the only
good argument – for Derrida's being a philosopher, being taken
to be or taken for a philosopher, at any rate, or being accepted *as*
a philosopher by those who are confident they really are philosophers, would be the presence *of* arguments – in the more noble
sense – in his texts. Leave a certain amount of Derrida to literary

[3] *Encyclopédie philosophique universelle* (Paris: PUF, 1990), vol II, article 'Argument', pp. 156-7.
[4] This turns out to be a good deal more complex than the Encyclopedia in question is able to say, for in fact the term 'argumentum' in both Cicero and Quintilian covers a wide and complex range, from *logos* in the Aristotelian sense I have mentioned, to proof, to enthymeme and epicheireme to summary to doubtful sign or indication. But it appears to be true that the unity of the term as used here comes from the drive to persuasion as conceived by rhetoric.

types (call it style, or something of that sort, the 'sharp tang of Gallic prose', as I seem to remember David Cooper has it – not very philosophically, perhaps – in his book on metaphor), but extract or distil from it the arguments, and then maybe it can be taken as philosophy. This will involve some re-writing and some more or less aggressive translation, and will typically give rise to 'arguments' which are not, and could not be, presented as quotations from Derrida, but as somehow contained in or implied by his texts, so that when he says things like 'there is nothing outside the text', or 'a letter always might not arrive at its destination', the transcription might retain none of the words of the original formulation at all, but perhaps say things such as: 'there is no being that is not constitutively defined or identified by reference to other beings' (for the first case), or, for the second: 'meaning is such that it must be possible for it to be mistaken by its intended addressee (and indeed any addressee at all)' or even, more ambitiously, 'what have usually been construed as contingent failures affecting an action or process must be thought of as positive conditions of possibility – but thereby also impossibility – of that action or process' (though we might then be at something of a loss to know what to make of the fact that this latter transcription could also reasonably be arrived at from what Derrida says about Austin and performatives in 'Signature, Event, Context' and what he formulates perhaps more straightforwardly *as* an argument in 'Limited Inc a b c...', where Derrida writes, for example, of 'an iterability that ruins (even ideally) the identity it makes possible' (Derrida 1988, pp. 144–5)). This process of transcription might then be taken to produce an 'improved' Derrida – perhaps in the sense in which polite society in the Morningside district of Edinburgh used to talk of cats being taken to the vet to be 'improved'. And arguments in this sense, the sense in which one might ask 'what's the argument?' of an essay or book or piece of reasoning, are probably indeed the ones that most concern us here today. If Derrida is to be accepted into the fold of philosophers, *recognised* by those philosophers who believe they really are philosophers and know what philosophy really is and how to do it,[5]

[5] Cf. Dummett's *Origins of Analytical Philosophy* (London: Duckworth, 1993) which opens its first chapter with something like (I have only been able to consult the French translation of the German version of this text): 'What distinguished analytic philosophy in its various aspects from other philosophical currents is primarily the conviction that a philosophical analysis of language can lead to a philosophical explanation of thought, and in second place the conviction that this is the only way to achieve a global explanation'.

then he will have to put up arguments, or, if he is disinclined so to do, others will have to find the arguments in his texts and present them for him. And 'argument' in this sense would mean something like a sequence of related propositions tending to establish the validity of a position or a thesis of some sort. My sense is that the most common perception of Derrida among his Anglo-Saxon philosophical readers is that there are plenty of theses or apparent theses in Derrida (such as, for example, 'There is nothing outside the text', 'Perception does not exist', 'Everything that is, is in deconstruction', 'In the beginning was the telephone', and so on), but an idea that these theses are not properly backed up by argument. I think that this is a largely mistaken perception, motivated by a number of more or less bad reasons, and that it is perfectly possible, *up to a point*, to find and state arguments in Derrida, and have spent a fair amount of my academic time doing just that, more or less conscientiously, more or less, but perhaps not very, philosophically, more or less parodically, as again here today. There is probably no very *immediately* compelling reason why a volume on Derrida should not figure, for example, in that eminent series called 'The Arguments of the Philosophers' (though I have no idea if in fact such a volume is planned).

My concern today, however, is less to do with just what arguments this 'method' might be able successfully to extract from the thousands of pages of Derrida's tangy and Gallic prose, nor how they relate to each other (so that some might be versions of others, or there might be a more or less systematic hierarchical ordering to be made of them, or even one master-argument – probably indeed something about necessary possibility – to be taken as Derrida's main contribution to philosophy, his major argument on which all the others would depend) and more to do with what is happening in this process or procedure of transcription or translation. What more or less implicit theory of *reading* (we are, after all, hosted here by the University of Reading) is at work when this is the form the output takes? What I'd like to be able to argue – and I like arguing, I just love arguments – is that this type of approach (and 'analytic' seems not a bad word for it, though I believe the expression 'analytic philosophy' is currently controversial in Anglo-American circles) is not at all interested in reading as such (just because it wants to get the arguments out), and that this lack of interest in reading leads it to a practice of reading (for it can hardly avoid reading altogether) which is fated to be blind to just those features of language (but not just of

language) that Derrida is most concerned to bring out, non-argu-
mentatively (and perhaps not very philosophically: I have tried to
argue on occasion that deconstruction is the least philosophical
discourse imaginable, although it also often *looks just like* philosophy, that it is perhaps not very philosophical by virtue of being so
very philosophical – so in a sense philosophers do indeed recognise Derrida at their peril, and at the peril of their discipline and
its more or less rigorously – or at least jealously – guarded fron-
tier). I think that this relation to reading is not an accident, but
flows quite straightforwardly from an over-riding concern with
argument – for what is argument in this sense if not *logos*? – and a
way of thinking that is occupied with the *extraction* of arguments
(like the extraction of teeth, perhaps, or of confessions) is always
likely to exhibit those features that Derrida, since his earliest
work, has been concerned to diagnose under the name of logocentrism. And one of the salient features of Derrida's work that
would probably go missing in this 'argued' form would have to do
with its *occasions*, its dramatising of iterability by the very manner
in which the 'same' argument returns, and must be read, each
time differently.

There are two broad ways of presenting this situation, I think.
One way thinks of it as a contest or war: on this view there is logocentrism (or argumento-centrism) on the one side, and something else (style, literature, Heidegger, 'the continent', 'the
reflections of philosophical sages or prophets, such as Pascal and
Nietzsche, and... the obscurities of speculative metaphysicians,
such as Hegel, Bradley or Heidegger', as P.M.S. Hacker has it,
perhaps not very philosophically[6]) on the other, and these two
sides really have to fight it out. I believe that this has been the
dominant way in which these matters have been presented. And
as is not unusual in situations of warfare, the sides will often find
it to their advantage to adopt strategic means to achieve certain
ends – so we might expect propaganda of various sorts to be used
at various levels of the conflict, from published polemics and
denunciations and even smears, to departmental manoeuvrings
and even the way academic appointments are made (it is often
hard for me to write references for my students when the adver-
tisement specifies expertise in traditional divisions of Anglo-
Saxon philosophy as desiderata for applicants: 'philosophy of

[6] P.M.S. Hacker, *Wittgenstein's Place in Twentieth-Century Analytic Philosophy* (Oxford: Blackwell, 1996), p. 3.

mind', for example – I do not really know what 'philosophy of mind' is, and indeed one reason I was keen to come today was to try to find out – and so it is often hard for them to get very far with applications to departments of philosophy). Much of the discussion in this area has been of this polemical, war-driven sort – and this is, I think, rather massively the case on the 'analytic' side (examples could be cited here if necessary, though I suppose the name 'Cambridge' might stand here as a handy, if slightly brutal, metonym). And this need not be surprising if it is true that the analytic side is the one committed to argument as *logos*: tending therefore to perceive its opponents as irrational (in one way or another) this side will easily believe itself to be authorised by reason itself to operate all manner of exclusions and condemnations. Nothing is more like a holy war than the war of what perceives itself as reason against what it perceives as unreason (holy wars, for example).

I do not think that this is a helpful way of presenting the situation. But I do not say this just because of a vaguely liberal sense of tolerance or of the superior virtues of discussion. I do not think we make much progress in rejecting the thought of two sides in conflict if we merely replace it with the more comforting thought of two sides in *discussion* – the model of discussion as a rational substitute for conflict is one worthy of our deep suspicion, I think (at least in these academic matters). Let's fight if we must, and let's discuss if we must, but let's not think that the latter will necessarily solve the problems that gave rise to the former. Discussion, *pace* Habermas (but 'pace' here, as usual in academic contexts, really means something more like its opposite), is war continued by other means.

The other way of construing the situation is to cast doubt on the very presentation of it *as* a conflict. I want to suggest that nothing is more logocentric than the presentation of the relation of Derrida's thought (or deconstruction more generally) to ('analytic') philosophy as a relation of critique, conflict or warfare. The point (but it is a point I really do think it is easier to approach from the deconstructive side, as it were, and that is why there is still a polemical edge to what I am saying) is not to take sides and see who can win, but to rethink the relation between 'argument' and, say, 'text' (or 'writing') in a non-oppositional and non-conflictual way (or at least a non-confrontational way – I certainly do not mean to imply anything very irenic here: let's not simply take refuge in *politesse*). This is not to suggest that there are no differences between what are no longer quite two sides, but that (and perhaps just this would be the main 'argument' of deconstruction) the multifarious differences between and within each side are being grossly (violently) simplified when they are presented as always finding their truth in opposition and confrontation – this being deconstruction's point of difference with Hegelian dialectics and everything that Hegel sums up (even in analytic philosophy, I imagine) about reason's way with difference. The advantages of construing the situation in this differential-but-non-oppositional way are many – and notably that it remains possible to use (and indeed to believe in) arguments *up to a point*. Deconstruction is not against arguments, not allergic to them, but uses them always *up to a point*. (I think Adrian Moore will quote Derrida claiming that the quasi-concept of *différance* 'exceeds the order of truth at a very precise point'.) *Up to a point* here does not mean that after that point one no longer believes in argument, or that argument only serves to bring one to that point whereafter argument can be joyfully or tragically dispensed with – rather that argument can help (or perhaps can't help, can't help itself) to establish the (local) limits of its own validity.

I call this a re-construal because it emphatically does not mean that we divide up the field into argument on the one hand and 'style' on the other, with a more or less sharp or blurred boundary between them – because just that is the way that *argument* construes the situation. (This is like most arguments over the relationship between philosophy and literature, which tend to presuppose the sort of distinction they are supposed to be establishing: it is probably already a philosophical gesture to ask about the boundary between philosophy and literature – so when Habermas criticises Derrida for effacing that boundary he is simply and dogmatically asserting the primacy of the philosophical and missing the point entirely.) The 'field' here has to be thought of as differentiated in a more complex way than the endemically territorial, frontier-defined way we probably inherited from Kant (maybe fractal geometry, or something like the Australian Aboriginal understanding of space as essentially to do with lines and tracks might help – probably starting by calling it a field is already a source of trouble, and leads to the further trouble of talk of conceptual space, of concepts as having boundaries or frontiers, and so on: we would need here to have a careful look at Derrida's various formulations of the notion of 'closure', and the topology of what he calls 'invagination') – as more multifarious or multidimensional, not essentially confrontational or even argumentative, but not excluding local confrontational or argumentative moments either. I want to say that this enlarged or reconfigured 'field' is helpfully thought of in Derrida's sense as textual (indeed that the only helpful way of thinking about it is as 'textual'), and that argument has a real but limited – local – place within it.

III

What I am really interested in, though, is the thought that it is through argument itself that the limit of argument might be, what? – Argued? Established? Proven? Demonstrated? Suggested? *Mise en scène?* In other words, I am interested in concepts or structures which seem to lead to their own demise. But it looks as though there are two ways that this might happen. One is through teleological fulfilment, so that the thing in question *finishes itself off*. We might want to say, for example – I have often in fact said – that the end of politics is the end of politics: meaning that if politics (at least of the 'Grand Narrative' sort, as Lyotard would say) came to fruition or got to the end of itself and its projects, then there would be no more politics and no more need for politics – and I believe that just this is the structure of much political thought. Similarly, perhaps, with ethics: if ethics reached its end and we all became angels (or even humans, heaven forbid), there would be no more need for ethics, at least in the normal sense of the term. (A rather startling consequence of this thought is that what Kant calls 'radical evil' becomes a positive condition of ethics, what Derrida in recent years has developed as the thought (still perhaps within the ambit of the 'necessary possibility argument) of an essential, constitutive *pervertibility* of the ethical as part of its being-ethical, its condition of possibility and impossibility.) Structures of this type are familiar at least since Kant, and depend on what Kant designates with the word 'Idea'. An Idea, or concept of Reason, is one which draws its meaning from the fact of being out of reach, referring to an infinitely distant state that we are typically supposed to aim at asymptotically, so that the Idea both *gives* us a *telos* to aim at, and is predicated on that *telos's* remaining forever out of reach, forever unrealised, never in fact given at all. This is of course the sort of structure in Kant that leads to Hegel's derision, and more generally motivates the section of the latter's *Greater Logic* on 'The Limit and the Ought'.

In spite of Hegel's strictures, we still implicitly understand many things in this way, so that, for example, we might say that the end of discussion is the end of discussion – if the presumed *telos* of discussion, i.e. agreement, were ever reached, there would be no point continuing the discussion any further (imagine that – we might just decide we absolutely agree and go off for an early – and long – lunch…: I remember last year at Sussex I had a long and rather ill-tempered disagreement with an eminent visitor about whether the end of discussion really was to reach agreement, and our failure to come to an agreement about that led to a rather late – and consequently rather short – lunch. No one was happy.). I suspect that it is no accident that Derrida, especially in his early work on Husserl, pays a great deal of attention to this motif of the 'Idea in the Kantian sense' (at least as Husserl deploys it) – and it is also interesting that a very common misconstrual of what Derrida is doing involves normalising it on just the model of the Kantian Idea it is, I am sure, tending to disrupt. (Think for example of the way 'différance' has often been presented as an 'infinite deferral' of meaning.)

But there is another way of understanding this sort of situation. For if certain things or situations tend to fulfil themselves by finishing themselves off, then we might expect that the best way of maintaining such things or situations *against* that finishing off would be to interrupt, or disrupt in some way, that teleological progression towards fulfilment. (More accurately, and to avoid the excessive voluntarism of that way of putting it, the point would be to show up a sort of internal interruption or disruption of the teleology: it is not that we don't like it and so try to stop it, but rather that the teleology is always already marked by a constitutive falling short – and I believe that this can be shown already at work in Kant, beyond Kant's 'official' understanding of it.) So that if the end of discussion is the end of discussion, then we might want to say that discussion can be preserved *as* discussion, as itself, only by putting an end to that end, or at least by conniving in the maintenance of discussion *short of* its presumed end. (This is in fact just the point Lyotard is making against Habermas at the end of *The Postmodern Condition*, when he, rather disconcertingly, plays dissensus off against consensus.) So discussion would make sense, on this view, only to the extent that it remained unfulfilled in a way that was not provisional – discussion *never was* going to lead to agreement.

And indeed this very structure, and the concomitant thought

of two different 'ends', pervades Derrida's work from the start. (We might even be tempted to say that it is the same argument as the one I mentioned before about apparently contingent failures being conditions of possibility, and therefore impossibility). Think of the remarks about the concept of the sign in 'Structure, Sign and Play' or *Of Grammatology*, for example (where the argument goes, for it is still an argument up to a point: 'sign' is a metaphysical concept; this metaphysical concept of 'sign' is the concept of its own teleological reduction or disappearance in the presence of the thing signified; so we can do something to metaphysics by maintaining (now: *en maintenant maintenant* – deconstruction happens each time now) – by maintaining the sign short of that reduction or disappearance)), or think of the remarks about metaphor at the end of 'The White Mythology' (where the argument goes, similarly, and it is still an argument: the concept of metaphor is metaphysical in that it is the concept of metaphor's 'death' or effacement, its ending in the presence of proper meaning; but by maintaining metaphor short of that *telos* (i.e. its death as prescribed by philosophy) maybe we provoke the death *of* philosophy in a quasi-metaphorical textuality that never quite comes back down to proper meaning at all (whence 'dissemination', which philosophy will never get on top of).

Now I want to end by saying that this same structure affects the concept of argument too. (I claim no great merit for that suggestion, in that Derrida, in 'Structure, Sign and Play', says that what he is saying about the sign can be extended to all the concepts of metaphysics,[7] and the 'Plus de métaphore' section of 'The White Mythology' does something similar.) This seems certainly to be the case when 'argument' is taken in the sense of more or less heated discussion, according to the schema we have just seen – and indeed the word 'argument' helps to bring out what might seem paradoxical about this structure of discussion. People who enjoy arguments know the disappointment that can result from an argument coming to an end, even in victory – and parents know how adept children can be at keeping arguments going independently of any 'rational' outcome (but the structure of what is rational is itself at issue here). But I also want to suggest (or argue, why not?) that this also holds true of the more noble concept of 'argument' too. An argument in this stronger, more 'philosophical' sense, is a piece of reasoning that tends to a *conclu-*

---

[7] Jacques Derrida, *Writing and Difference*, trans. A. Bass (London: RKP, 1978) p. 279.

sion, but in that conclusion the argument *for* or *in favour of* that conclusion comes to an end (it is 'sublated', Hegel would say). But the conclusion is really *not* the interesting point at all (philosophical conclusions are mostly quite familiar already as *propositions*), and on its own just looks dogmatic and indeed, as Flaubert said (and as Derrida discusses), *stupid* ('That's what's stupid about philosophy, that's its stupidity, what makes it derisory and fascinating for Flaubert: it wants to conclude... this essential stupidity of the philosophical...').[8] The argument may be *in favour of* a given conclusion, but the *point* of doing philosophy is surely not to come to a conclusion about the great issues (Does the external world exist? Are there other minds? Is there a God? and so on), because those conclusions are so familiar and, in themselves, *as* conclusions, so uninteresting. Imagine the banner headlines in the tabloids: 'Philosophers conclude that external world exists'; 'Philosophers conclude there really are other minds'; or even 'Philosophers conclude that there is nothing outside the text' – the point of doing philosophy, *pace* early Wittgenstein, is *not* to *solve* philosophical problems, nor, *pace* later Wittgenstein, so that I can stop doing philosophy (so that the end of philosophy would be the end of philosophy – see Wittgenstein 1958, §133[9]), but so that I can entertain and deploy arguments which tend towards such or such a conclusion, rather than *reaching* that conclusion itself.

But of course the concept of argument (in this sense) is, as it comes down to us, inseparable from that of conclusion, so that an argument thought of in this radically argumentative way, always *short of* its conclusion, stops looking quite so much like an argument and more like something else. What? Well, an *argument*. Just as a sign maintained against its self-effacement looks just like a sign, more and more like a sign; just as a metaphor held short of its philosophical death in the concept looks just like a metaphor, more and more like a metaphor, so an argument held short of a conclusion looks just like an argument – and even more like an

---

[8] Jacques Derrida, *Psyché: inventions de l'autre* (Paris: Galilée, 1987), p. 309. Translation mine.

[9] 'For the clarity we are aiming at is indeed *complete* clarity. But this simply means that the philosophical problems should *completely* disappear.

   The real discovery is the one that makes me capable of stopping doing philosophy when I want to. – The one that gives philosophy peace . . . '
Ludwig Wittgenstein, *Philosophical Investigations*, trans. G.E.M. Anscombe (Oxford: Blackwell, 1958), §133.

argument than it ever did, a sort of hyper-reality of argument. (I would like to suggest that this situation introduces some interesting new issues into philosophy, such as the question of the *speed* of reading and arguing: how *fast* is a good argument?) This curious sort of liberating of argument from its traditional *telos* (but also from the *telos* of liberation itself, of course) is what I think Derrida does. Derrida has an argument with argument, if you like, but that argument does not involve simply denying, criticising or even ignoring the claims of argument, but rather *loving* argument (who else ever entertained others' arguments as lovingly as Derrida?),[10] loving it, perhaps, unto death, and beyond. Perhaps this is not very philosophical.

DISCUSSION

John Cottingham: Thank you very much. Well, we now have some time for questions – or argument!

Philip Stratton-Lake: You suggest that there is a certain structure to both argument and ethics, namely, that they are both, in a certain way, self-undermining: that the end of argument is, as you put it, the end of argument, and that the end of ethics is the end of ethics. The idea here is that argument and ethics have no use once they achieve their goal. I was not convinced by this because I do not think that the aim of argument and ethics is mere agreement, and thus do not believe that they necessarily come to an end when we reach agreement, irrespective of what we agree about. For example, we might come to agree by argument on a certain view, and also agree that that view has certain problems with it. Here we have reached agreement, but there is clearly more to be argued. The same is true for ethical discourse. We may come to agree on a set of values through moral deliberation and argument, but also come to agree that these values do not cohere. Thus, while we have reached agreement on moral issues there is still an awful lot more for moral discourse to debate. So I just wasn't convinced by this structure – that the end of argument and ethics is the end of argument and ethics. Argument and ethics are not, I believe, really about combat and

[10] Cf. Jacques Derrida, 'Pour l'amour de Lacan' in *Résistances de la psychanalyse* (Paris: Galilée, 1996).

winning, but about something more noble, that is, the true and
the good; though that probably sounds rather pompous.
Geoffrey Bennington: No, not at all! Thank you. That's helpful
because it means that I hadn't been as clear as I had hoped. What
I was saying, and trying to draw some analogies about the structure of, was this: that the end of discussion was traditionally
thought to be agreement; the end of argument was traditionally
thought to be something like the establishing of a conclusion
(that may not straightforwardly just be an issue of reaching
agreement, of course, though the two may well have a relation);
and (in perhaps a far too off-hand way) that the end of ethics
wouldn't be to reach agreement, but that if the end of ethics were
reached, in the sense of all of us becoming ethical (*whatever* that
might mean, and whatever the state of our intervening agree-
ments or disagreements about it), then it would stop having a
point. So I didn't mean to make *agreement* the end of all those
different things. I especially didn't want to say that the traditional
concept of ethics reaches its end in agreement. Nor that the traditional concept of argument reaches its end in agreement. I
wanted to say that the traditional concept of discussion reaches its
end in agreement; the traditional concept of argument reaches its
end in conclusion; and the traditional concept of ethics reaches
its end in, well, ethics. And that there was some analogy possible
between those structures. But agreement wasn't supposed to be
the dominant term for thinking in each case of what the end
would involve.
Eric Woehrling: The word you use in French as the equivalent of
arguing is '*arguer*', but in French there is another important word,
'*explication*', which also carries some of the same connotations as
argument. '*S'expliquer avec quelqu'un*' means 'to have it out with
them' (combative). But '*Explication de texte*' is also what the French
will use for 'close' (sensitive) reading. This ambiguity was helpful
in translating Heidegger's '*Auseinandersetzung*', an expression
which means both to argue and to explain. Still, we can say that
the translation of '*Auseinandersetzung*' by '*explication*' is also a kind
of 'arguing': the translation is itself an 'explicative' process. But
the point is that with the word '*explication*', the combative sense of
having an argument, which you outlined as one side of the
debate, and the other sense – explaining what somebody else is
saying – the other side of the debate, are both implicit in each
other. And this is important for deconstruction. For what I understand deconstruction to be doing when it is reading another text

is saying what that text is saying but in its '*différance*' from itself. Thus, for example, the critique of Rousseau's logocentrism is found 'within' what Rousseau himself is saying. In the light of this, it is perhaps problematic that Derrida's use of this word '*explication*' is translated as 'confrontation' and a similar French word '*solliciter*' (when Derrida says, in *Of Grammatology*, 'the movement of deconstruction does not solicit the structures of metaphysics from the outside') is translated by Spivak as 'destroy', ('do not destroy the structures of metaphysics . . . ').

So there are two points here. First, I didn't get the sense that the notion of argument you wanted to affirm was implicit in the other (combative) sense of argument which you were critiquing – a movement of reading which is important in deconstruction. And, second, I wonder how far you think English translations of words like '*expliquer*' and '*solliciter*' have contributed to the misrepresentation of Derrida's views on things like 'arguing' in deconstruction.

Geoffrey Bennington: On the second point, the question of the English translation of Derrida's work is a huge issue, and it's a complex one. It is absolutely true (and I say this with some trepidation, obviously) that many of the English translations of Derrida – why not? – *all* the English translations of Derrida are seriously deficient in various ways. The example you give from Spivak on that particular point is one example, and we could give many more. (I've given examples on occasion of more or less gross mistranslations.) Now, just on the question of translation, which I'm not sure is the main issue here, I think that in principle you're right: everything you say about the notions of '*expliquer*' and '*explication*' is helpful. Having said that, we don't want to fall into a sense that 'the French have a word for it' – that view of the French language as so much more subtle, with that special *je ne sais quoi!* The resources of terms like '*explication*' are not 'in them' like something 'in' a box. It depends on how they are deployed in a way I think that Derrida would call 'syntactic'. If you like, it depends on the 'grammar' of those words as they are deployed across his text.

'*Auseinandersetzung*' is of course another huge issue in itself and that could take us quite a long way away. The reason that I talked about 'argument' (and '*arguer*') is that that is the word in the title that Simon Glendinning gave us for the conference. And because it is a nicely and richly ambiguous title, I was able to concentrate on that in this context. But, of course, '*explication*' is an interesting

and in many ways more fruitful way of describing Derrida's relation with other texts than 'argument'. I think that's right.
Christina Howells: I think I followed you when you were talking
and, on the whole, even if you were not arguing, your speech went
slowly enough for the stages to be fairly clear. Except at one point:
when you were talking about ethics and the condition of possibility of ethics, 'radical evil' suddenly jumped in. Could you say a
little more about that please?
Geoffrey Bennington: Yes. Let me say first that I added that in
after having seen, in advance, the paper Adrian Moore will give
today, in which he quotes Derrida saying that the confusion of
use and mention may well be an instance (at least) of evil, or
perhaps even evil itself. That is what prompted me to throw in a
remark about radical evil. What does it mean here? It is related
to but does not quite have the sense that Kant gave it. I think I
said, as I often say, '*Something like* radical evil'. (And that kind of
gesture is obviously part of the 'not very philosophical'
sequence in the paper.) It is 'radical' because, in the way of
thinking I am outlining, it is not being placed in the context of
its overcoming, or removal. That is, it is 'radical' in that it is 'in
from the start' and is ineradicable. This takes us back to the
question of the 'end of ethics'. As I said, 'ethics' is traditionally
taken to be a move towards its achievement, an achievement of
an ethical situation. This situation is envisaged by Kant on various occasions and in slightly different ways. But the basic idea is
that it would be one where the moral law would no longer be
expressed as a command: there would be no need, or there
would be no possibility, for the moral law to be expressed as a
prescription. At that point in fact, the very distinction between
descriptive law and prescriptive law would simply evaporate,
they would be the same thing: prescriptive laws would have
disappeared into descriptive laws. Now, if you want to think
about ethics in a broadly Kantian way, but also want to recognise
the force of the Hegelian critique (which is partly a critique
based on that logic of 'the end of ethics' and what Hegel thinks
is absurd about it), then ethics depends for its survival *as* ethics
on the maintenance of the *possibility* of all the things that hold it
short of that notional fulfilment. And the idea of 'radical evil' is
a quick way of invoking that. We can come back to this in the
context of what Adrian Moore will say. In that context, if 'radical evil' is partly about the necessary *possibility* of the confusion
of use and mention, then the point is that to the extent that that

possibility *is* necessary – and even necessary for ethics to be ethics – then it is not going to disappear.

John Cottingham: I wonder if I could raise something about what you said towards the end about the liberation of argument from its traditional *telos*. I thought that was an interesting idea, but I'm not sure that I am quite convinced about the kind of liberation you have in mind. It seems true that many conclusions which philosophers reach, stated on their own, might be rather dreary or banal or 'stupid' to use Flaubert's expression, but it could remain true nonetheless that argument is teleological in the sense that it is directed towards the reaching of a conclusion, and there could still be value in the way that conclusion is arrived at.

Geoffrey Bennington: Of course, of course, yes. At the end of my paper, probably too quickly, I tried to make a distinction, which I didn't thematise, between a 'liberating of argument' that would-n't quite be the same as a 'liberation of argument'. What I was trying to capture by that was the thought that, if having said what I'd said, I quickly said 'So that's a liberation of argument', that falls straight back into the sort of teleological structures I was trying to say something about and complicate. The point is that if I am inclined to talk about a 'liberating of argument', I then have, on my own construals, to hold that short of a *telos* in 'liberation' where argument would be completely liberated from conclusions. I don't want to do that! I want to maintain argument, as I say, 'up to a point', and argument as we inherit it is always going to have a teleological drift. That is not something to be sneered at or discounted. So when you say there might still be some interest or validity in the way the conclusion is reached – well, that's fine. That's, in a way, what I am also suggesting: that the interest – and the 'validity' if you like – is short of the end, it's not what happens at the end.

Let me be clear that I don't mean this as an attack on the argu-mentative protocols of analytic philosophy. It is also absolutely true in deconstructive thinking as well. One of the temptations that students encountering Derrida's work often fall into, and not only students (I think this was perhaps more true in the earlier years of that reception than it is now) was to reach conclusions *too quickly*. And the conclusion would be something like 'So it's all writing' or 'So it's all text'. This is just as 'stupid', just as *formally* 'stupid' (Flaubert's notion of stupidity is not really about the content of the conclusion, it's the form of conclusion or conclusiveness that is taken to be 'stupid') as any other conclusion. This is also what motivated the remark I made at the end about speed. How fast do you argue, how fast do you track through the '*explication*' (to use the term that was suggested)? Because, in a way, you can go very fast with deconstruction, as students are tempted to do. Then, of course, they find that it's not very interesting. If you have a half page of discussion of something and then quickly conclude 'So it's all text – isn't it?', that's hopeless. The question is how the unfolding (that is also what '*explication*' is a nice term for) of the argument is conducted. But I would not want to suggest either that this is never thought about or accounted for or practised within what you could call 'analytic philosophy'.

John Cottingham: In raising the question, I was thinking in particular of Socrates, who famously talked about following the argument where it leads (which is a highly teleological notion) but didn't actually assert many conclusions.

Geoffrey Bennington: Yes, but really it's only ambiguously teleological. I mean 'following the argument where it leads' might mean it leads 'nowhere', in a certain sense of 'nowhere'. Of course, introducing this complication isn't meant to imply that argument is not *really* teleological. Dummett, in his book on Frege, talks about sense and reference and construes sense as 'the route to the reference'. In his discussion he makes the point that some 'routes' lead nowhere. Of course, 'literally' this is nonsense. Any road leads somewhere. It might be 'the middle of nowhere', but it is still somewhere. But this complication doesn't simply ruin Dummett's point. Equally, while the notion of argument *is* teleological one can also talk about 'an argument leading nowhere'. It isn't senseless. (Incidentally, I wonder whether Socrates really can be said to follow arguments where they lead, rather than where he wants them to go, but that's another issue.) There are many remarks in Derrida about following one's nose and *not knowing* where one is going, and I think that this is already the kind of complication of the teleological structures I was trying to bring out.

Jacques Derrida: As you can imagine, it is very difficult to intervene at this point. But let me take advantage of this moment to say, first of all, to Professor Cottingham and to Simon Glendinning – and to Geoff – how grateful I am for being received in the way I am. It really is a moving occasion for me. You see, it occurs a long, long time after another one, that I would like briefly to recall, when I delivered the lecture on *différance*, not far from here, in Oxford, in 1967. I was totally mad to go to Oxford then to give that lecture! On that occasion the *silence* which followed it was obviously eloquent. Eloquently saying: 'There is no arguing here and there is no prospect of arguing with this man, or with this discourse.' Strawson was there – and very politely kept silent. Ryle was there – didn't say a word. It was very embarrassing for me, a very embarrassing situation. Ayer started arguing – but it didn't improve the situation. So that was more than thirty years ago, and I know that this afternoon the lecture on *différance* will be discussed again, and I feel all the more grateful.

And I feel guilty. Guilty for the length of time it has taken. Guilty because I did not make the effort that most of you are making, with moving good will, just to produce the possibility of 'an argument' (whatever that may mean, and Geoff has, as usual, given the most powerful and most brilliant account of everything that can be said around this word). Guilty because I didn't make the effort to read, when I should have read, 'analytic' or 'Anglo-Saxon' or 'British' philosophy; an effort which could have helped this discussion, this argument or dialogue. For example, this after-noon I will be asked 'Why don't you mention Wittgenstein?' And I have no justification for that. Simply: *I failed.*

So I feel guilty. And particularly so since the possibility of 'argu-ing with' or 'between' us opened here, promises the chance not for a polemical discussion (which it may look or sound like) but a way of reconciliation. For even the *prospect* of arguing was already to recognise that arguing was possible. It means, already, if not the beginning of 'an agreement' then at least of 'a recon-ciliation'. In French we use the word '*conciliation*' when after or at the eve of a divorce we try nevertheless to make discussion possi-ble again. And I am thinking too of the 'truth and reconciliation commission' in South Africa. For I feel that we are, on this moving occasion, in a 'truth and reconciliation commission'! This after-noon the question of truth will come back very strongly, and I'll do my best to address the question of truth. But now, following the model of the truth and reconciliation commission where, under the authority of Bishop Tutu, reconciliation supposes that the guilty one *confess*, I confess! And then we'll see for the truth! And, in the sessions that follow, however unable I may be to really respond to the questions and objections posed to me, however weak I may be in the discussion, I'm sure that this will be an important step. In 'the middle of nowhere' perhaps! But an important step. Towards...I don't know what!

Now, I would like to try to connect these words of gratitude to my hosts with what was said a moment ago about teleology and about radical evil. I have often confessed that I could not not say, as Geoff recalled, that the end or *telos* of anything was always also its end or demise; that the teleological accomplishment of an argument or discussion will be simply its end or destruction. But, nevertheless, I could also not not accept being involved in the teleological movement. To say that the fulfilment of the *telos* is the end doesn't mean that we could simply free ourselves from the teleology. So I often speak of a teleology or strategy 'with no end'. We are organising a discussion, we multiply arguments or reasons, '*ratio*', '*rationes*', but knowing that at the end not only is there no end but that there *should* be no end – that the end would be the death of the teleology itself. That is the internal contradiction within the structure of teleology.

Perhaps the logical matrix of this argument will surface again this afternoon. It certainly cannot be dissociated from what was called 'radical evil'. To recall, the thought of 'radical evil' here is not concerned with it as an eventuality. It is simply that the *possibility* of something evil, or of some corruption, the *possibility* of the non-accomplishment, or of some failure, is *ineradicable*. And it is so because it is the condition for every felicity, every positive value – the condition for ethics for instance. So, if you want to eradicate the *possibility* of this negative then you destroy what you want to save. Thus ethics couldn't be ethical without the ineradicable *possibility* of evil. (That's why it is not simply Kantian – although it has something to do with Kant.) The *possibility* of infelicity, non-fulfilment, is part of what it is that we want to save under the name of ethics, politics, felicity, fulfilment, and so on.

For me this concept of possibility, of possibility as something which has to be saved at the moment that it may ruin what we want to save, this 'possibility as impossibility', is the most unavoidable argument today. I use the word 'argument' in the sense of something which can be used in a logical demonstration as something convincing. I want to convince. Geoff has said everything that has to be said about one sense of argumentation as a way of demonstrating and convincing at the same time, and showing the unavoidability of reasoning, of *ratio*. Well, I would say that this thought of 'possibility as impossibility' is the 'final argument' in the logic of the discussion we are going to have. In my current work I am struggling with the *history* of these concepts of possibility and impossibility. (Geoff noted that the notions of argument and arguing, which are so rich in English – but there is a question of translation which will haunt us today – has a history. The same is true for the concepts of possibility and impossibility.) I am trying to interrogate the tradition of the concepts of possibility and impossibility that we are inheriting, trying to free it, or rather, to go a little further than what, in transcendental philosophy and elsewhere, we usually understand by these words. In particular, I am trying to think how the only possible *x* should occur under the form of the impossible. For instance, that the only possible hospitality (I come back to hosts and hospitality here) is a hospitality which wouldn't be simply an invitation in which the host opens his house, his language, his problematic, only to the extent, or up to the point, that the guest respects the rules, and so on. Hospitality is not just an invitation but must allow for a *visitation* – when you are surprised by the unexpected guest that might ruin the house. But, of course, in that case hospitality is impossible. It is impossible to accept in advance that the guest may enter the house and undermine or destroy or subvert everything in your own order. Yet this is the only possible hospitality: the impossible hospitality. The only possible hospitality is a hospitality that does the impossible, is open to the impossible. I would say exactly the same for the gift. I would say exactly the same for forgiveness. The only possible forgiveness is the impossible forgiveness. So I am trying to elaborate a logic, and I would call this a 'logic', in which the only possible *x* (and I mean here any *rigorous concept* of *x*) is 'the impossible *x*'. And to do so without being caught in an absurd, nonsensical discourse. For instance, the statement according to which the only possible gift is an impossible gift, is meaningful. Where I can give only what I am able to give, what it is possible for me to give, I don't give. So, for me to give something, I have to give something I don't have, that is, to make an impossible gift.

As I see it, this statement is *logically* irrefutable. That is why I love arguing! But we really need to come back here to this question of the 'logical' dimension of argumentation. Because all of these wars between, let us say, 'analytic philosophy' and so-called 'continental philosophy' (assuming that is that 'deconstruction' *is* 'continental' – we will come back to this later this afternoon), all of these wars around argumentation, have assumed that 'arguing' is fundamentally on the side of a *certain* logic. Yet when Heidegger used the word '*Auseinandersetzung*' and wouldn't translate this by 'discussion' or 'argument' or 'arguing', this was precisely because

in '*Auseinandersetzung*', in an '*explication avec quelqu'un*', there is
something more than a merely 'logistic' (in the narrow sense of
the word) duel. There is a French word that is missing in what I
have heard up to now: '*argutie*'. '*Argutie*' means '*ratiocination*', that
is, a certain modality of discussion in which *formal logic* or *formal
logicity* (not simply 'logic') is supposed to be the master that
controls the discussion. So the question is: when you ask questions about this logic, about precisely this 'controlling logistics',
are you simply 'illogical' or not? That is why Heidegger would
resist the translation of '*Auseinandersetzen*' by 'argumentation' in
the narrow sense of 'logic' as '*ratiocination*' or as '*argutie*'. But it is
also why it may be possible to say that one can 'argue' or have a
'rational argument' about the history of argument and the
history of logic, even the history of truth, without simply escaping
the problems in a sphere of obscure irrationality or non-logicity.
It is this leap *beyond a certain logic within logic* which I try to
perform and which is so difficult to perform.

SESSION TWO

Jonathan Dancy (chair): In this session we are going to have a paper by Adrian Moore of St. Hugh's College, Oxford. Adrian Moore has written extensively on the topics of infinity and the ineffable. In his most recent book *Points of View*, he has explored the possibility of whether we can form 'absolute representations': representations of the world which are not simply representations from our point of view. Today he has very kindly agreed to offer an appreciation, perhaps from his point of view, of certain arguments in the work of Derrida. Fittingly, his paper is called 'Arguing with Derrida'.

ARGUING WITH DERRIDA

A. W. Moore

1.

My brief today is to give my reaction to some selected arguments from the work of Derrida. I shall try to follow this brief by relating two of Derrida's best known texts, 'Différance' and 'Signature, Event, Context',[1] to some of my own interests and concerns. But first, I want to say a few words about the particular profile that I bring to this task.

2.

It is no secret that there are philosophers who deride the work of Derrida. There are those indeed who think that it is pernicious. I unequivocally distance myself from either category. However, although I greatly admire Derrida's work, I can claim no special expertise in it. The reaction to his work that I shall offer today, though it is not the reaction of an antagonist, *is* the reaction of an outsider.

---

[1] Both in Jacques Derrida, *Margins of Philosophy*, trans. Alan Bass (Brighton: Harvester Press, 1982).

58   A. W. MOORE

Very well then; a reaction from where outside?

Roughly speaking, the style of philosophy of which I take myself to be an exponent has as its principal aim clarity of understanding and as its principal methodological tool the analysis of concepts.[2] In an earlier version of this essay I unashamedly referred to this as 'analytic philosophy'.[3] But Simon Glendinning convinced me that this was unhelpful. For one thing, I was needlessly taking a stance in the controversy about how that label should be applied. But more importantly, given the connotations that the label has (and in particular, given the clumsy distinction that is often drawn between 'analytic philosophy' and 'continental philosophy'), I was implying that what followed was going to be part of some interchange between two philosophical 'fronts', perhaps even that it was going to contribute to hostilities between these two 'fronts' – which is not at all what I intend. Still, it would be useful to have *a* label for what I am talking about. So I shall appropriate the phrase 'conceptual philosophy' for this purpose, in the hope that, given this disclaimer, it will not carry the same unwelcome implications.

Now it is natural to characterize this style of philosophy – the style of philosophy that I am calling conceptual philosophy – by contrasting it with science. In particular, it is natural to dissociate it from the pursuit of knowledge or truth that scientists typically arrogate to themselves. Thus exponents of conceptual philosophy might say that it is not their business to discover and state truths about the world; rather, they aim to get into sharp focus various concepts, in particular concepts that bemuse us in certain distinctive ways, which are themselves used in discovering and stating truths about the world. If, in the course of doing this sort of philosophy, one makes any claims about reality, then it will be by way of demonstrating how these concepts work. The claims one makes will as likely as not be platitudes or items of common empirical knowledge. They will have no special significance of their own.[4]

---

[2] By the analysis of concepts I mean something very diverse. It encompasses on the one hand the use of formal techniques to demonstrate ways in which concepts come together, and on the other hand the creative use of the imagination to demonstrate ways in which they come apart.

[3] Cf. the characterizations of analytic philosophy offered in Michael Dummett, *Origins of Analytical Philosophy* (Cambridge: Harvard University Press, 1994) and P.M.S. Hacker, *Wittgenstein's Place in Twentieth-Century Analytic Philosophy* (Oxford: Basil Blackwell, 1996), in each case *passim.*

[4] Cf. Ludwig Wittgenstein, *Tractatus Logico-Philosophicus*, trans. D.F. Pears and B.F. McGuiness (London: Routledge & Kegan Paul, 1961), 4.111–4.116; Ludwig Wittgenstein,

While I applaud the spirit of this way of characterizing conceptual philosophy, I query the letter of it. There are certainly important distinctions between the practice of conceptual philosophy
and the practice of science. But I do not think it is helpful to
express these in terms of the pursuit of knowledge. There are
many ways of knowing things. Having a clear grasp of concepts
seems to me to be one of them. Someone who has a clear grasp
of a given family of concepts knows how to handle them; knows
what it is for them to apply; knows his or her way around a particular part of conceptual space. So I do not think that conceptual
philosophy should be dissociated fróm the pursuit of knowledge.
It is a different question whether it should be dissociated from the
pursuit of truth. Not all knowledge consists in the possession of
truth. This is an exceedingly important point to which I shall
return. But even if having a clear grasp of concepts is a case in
point (that is, even if having a clear grasp of concepts is a case of
knowing something without thereby being in possession of any
truth), the primary way of achieving and displaying such a grasp
will still be through the affirmation of truths. Conceptual philosophy may not involve the pursuit of truth in the way in which
science does; but there is an important sense, it seems to me, in
which conceptual philosophy has a *commitment* to the truth. A
conceptual philosopher is as beholden to eschew that which is
either false or nonsensical as a scientist is.[5]

3.

What I have said so far has involved all sorts of presuppositions
that are open to challenge. But I shall not attempt to defend it. I
have said it just to indicate where I am coming from.

Philosophical Investigations, trans. G.E.M. Anscombe (Oxford: Basil Blackwell, 1974),
§§122–133; Michael Dummett, 'Can Analytical Philosophy be Systematic, and Ought it to
Be?', reprinted in his *Truth and Other Enigmas* (London: Duckworth, 1978), pp. 438 ff.; and
P.M.S. Hacker, *op. cit.*, pp.110ff. But note: this further illustrates why I do well to eschew
the label 'analytic philosophy' here. There are plenty of philosophers who standardly
count as analytic philosophers and who champion precisely the opposite view (the view
that philosophy is continuous with science). The best known of these is Quine: see e.g.
W.V. Quine, 'Two Dogmas of Empiricism', reprinted in his *From a Logical Point of View:
Logico-Philosophical Essays* (New York: Harper & Row, 1961).

   [5] There is also *a* level, it seems to me, at which a conceptual philosopher is as beholden
to eschew that which is either false or nonsensical as an artist is. However, I would be wary
of saying that this distinguishes conceptual philosophy from any other kind of philosophy.
The comparison with science, on the other hand – being concerned with conceptual
philosophy's primary or most suitable mode of expression – does.

There is, however, one dialectically significant question in this area that I do wish to broach, namely whether there are any grounds for the suspicion that conceptual philosophy (as I have just characterized it) fails even in its own terms. If so, then conceptual philosophers will obviously need some way of allaying this suspicion. But that is not my principal reason for wanting to broach the question, at least not in this context. Rather I think that broaching the question will direct us to some important points of contact between conceptual philosophy and the work of Derrida.

Why, then, might one think that conceptual philosophy fails even in its own terms? One of the most important reasons is encapsulated in a question which anyone who has studied the recent history of philosophy will know has much exercised those who think of themselves as analytic philosophers, namely:

Is the concept of a horse a concept?

Presented just like that, the question looks both absurd and trivial, a burlesque of a question. So let me begin by saying something about what the question means and why it arises.

It is Frege's question.[6] Frege is often said to be the father of analytic philosophy. Whatever the merits of that epithet, he is certainly of colossal importance to what I am calling conceptual philosophy. This is in part because of how many of its techniques of analysis he devised, in the course of developing his celebrated semantic theory. Now there are two linguistic categories that are crucial to this theory: that of a name; and that of a declarative sentence. By a name Frege means any singular noun-phrase that can be used to refer to a particular object, where the term 'object' is understood in the broadest way possible. Examples of names are 'Paris', 'this animal', 'the cube root of 8' and 'procrastination'. By a declarative sentence Frege means a sentence that can be used to say something true or false. Examples of declarative sentences are 'Paris is a bigger city than Oxford' and 'This animal is a horse'. Frege asks us to consider what results when a name is removed from a declarative sentence. For example, when 'Paris' is removed from 'Paris is a bigger city than Oxford', we get ' . . .

[6] Gottlob Frege, 'On Concept and Object', trans. P.T. Geach, in *Translations From the Philosophical Writings of Gottlob Frege*, eds P.T. Geach and Max Black (Oxford: Basil Blackwell, 1952). See also Michael Dummett, *Frege: Philosophy of Language* (London: Duckworth, 1980), pp. 211ff.

is a bigger city than Oxford'; and when 'this animal' is removed from 'This animal is a horse', we get ' . . . is a horse'. He calls what results a predicate, and he calls what a predicate can be used to refer to a concept. This suggests that ' . . . is a bigger city than Oxford' can be used to refer to the concept of a city that is bigger than Oxford, and ' . . . is a horse' can be used to refer to the concept of a horse. But there is a problem here. What kind of thing is a concept? It had better be something of a fundamentally different kind from an object, Frege insists. Otherwise declarative sentences would in effect just be lists, like 'Paris, New York'. This would mean that they could not be used to say anything true or false. However, if the term 'object' really is understood in the broadest way possible, then it is hard to see how we can resist the conclusion that concepts, so far from being fundamentally different in kind from objects, are themselves objects. The phrase 'the concept of a horse', for instance, has all the hallmarks of a name. Frege concedes this. He admits that the concept of a horse is an object. But he continues to insist that concepts and objects are heterogeneous. Hence his question: 'Is the concept of a horse a concept?' The only way he can see of escaping his predicament is by denying that it is.

This tangle seems to represent something of a crisis for conceptual philosophy. The attempt to devise techniques that will help us to come to a clearer understanding of how we think about the world seems only to generate new confusion. Not only that. It seems to embroil us in an issue that is scarcely worthy of philosophical attention. How can conceptual philosophy have any pretensions to be taken seriously if it leads to preoccupation with such an inconsequential self-inflicted minutia of semantics?

The second of these charges I think can be firmly resisted. Frege's question is not the quibble it appears. It relates to fundamental philosophical issues about the unity of thought and the unity of reality. There are direct connections between his question and Kant's transcendental project (to take one notable example).[7] Moreover, within a generation of Frege's raising and addressing his question, Wittgenstein in turn related it, in a quite

---

[7] Immanuel Kant, *Critique of Pure Reason*, trans. Norman Kemp Smith (London: Macmillan, 1933), A95–130 and, differently in the second edition, B129–169: see e.g. A129 in the former and B141–42 in the latter. Cf. also Plato, *Sophist*, 261c6–262e2; and Plutarch, *Platonic Questions*, X, 1011c.

extraordinary way, to what he called 'the problem of life' and its meaning.[8] There is a lot more to be said about this of course. But I shall not say any more about it now. Of much more concern than the charge of triviality is the first charge, the charge that Frege's question indicates new confusion that conceptual philosophy generates. For all Frege's heroics, denying that the concept of a horse is a concept, he seems to have been driven by his own semantic theory to couch it in a way in which it ought not to be couched. Frege realized this, and was famously prompted to write:

> By a kind of necessity of language, my expressions, taken literally, sometimes miss my thought; I mention an object, when what I intend is a concept. I fully realize that in such cases I was relying upon a reader who would be ready to meet me half-way – who does not begrudge a pinch of salt.[9]

Likewise Wittgenstein, having urged that there are things that in principle cannot be said, was forced to recognize his own work as an ill-begotten attempt to say some of these things, and was just as famously prompted to write:

> Anyone who understands me eventually recognizes [my propositions] as nonsensical, when he has used them – as steps – to climb up beyond them. (He must, so to speak, throw away the ladder after he has climbed up it.) . . . What we cannot speak about we must pass over in silence.[10]

If it is the fate of conceptual philosophers, when trying to come to a clearer understanding of how our thoughts relate to the world and when trying to express the insights that they thereby achieve, to do so in ways that either have entirely the wrong sense or have no sense at all, and if conceptual philosophers are, as I put it earlier, beholden to eschew that which is either false or nonsensical, then we do, after all, seem forced to conclude that conceptual philosophy fails even in its own terms.

4.

In fact, we seem forced to recognize a more general failure here,

---

[8] Ludwig Wittgenstein, *Tractatus Logico-Philosophicus*, 4.12–4.1213, 5.551–5.641, and 6.4–7.

[9] *Op. cit.*, p. 54.

[10] *Op. cit.*, 6.54–7. See also 4.1212 and 6.522.

the failure of conceptual philosophy to come to terms with the ineffable. For it looks as if we can, in the light of what has just been said, mount the following broad case against conceptual philosophy.

Wittgenstein was right: some things cannot be put into words. Moreover, some things that cannot be put into words are of the utmost philosophical importance. By treating affirmation of the truth as its sole primary mode of philosophical expression, conceptual philosophy prevents itself from reckoning with these things, so that there is a real question about its very claim to the title of philosophy. As for Frege's question, that merely demonstrates how, in spite and because of its own methodology, conceptual philosophy is sucked into contact with the ineffable. When Frege himself, somewhat desperately, denies that the concept of a horse is a concept, or when Wittgenstein produces what he later in the same book denounces as nonsense about 'logical form',[11] what each is doing, in effect, is unsuccessfully trying to talk about that ineffable unity – of language, of reality, and of language with reality – which makes it possible to talk about anything at all. And the fact that each escapes the charge of revealing how trivial the concerns of conceptual philosophy are serves only to accentuate the force of the other charge: that they both reveal how inadequate the resources of conceptual philosophy are to cope with what is philosophically important.

5.

It is here at last that I think we can see points of contact with the work of Derrida. This case against conceptual philosophy has certain clear echoes in Derrida's remarkable essay 'Différance'.[12] Among the countless things that are going on in this essay, one, clearly, is that Derrida is directing our attention to, and attempting to come to terms with, something that is in some important sense ineffable. What this sense is is a delicate question. We cannot say that 'the ineffable' here is what resists expression by *any* linguistic means. If we do, we fall foul of what Derrida achieves in the very writing of his essay. (This is a point to which

[11] *Ibid.*, 4.12ff.
[12] For an approach to Derrida very close to that which I am about to take, tracing out similar connections, see Graham Priest, *Beyond the Limits of Thought* (Cambridge: Cambridge University Press, 1995), Part 4, esp. Chs. 12 and 14.

I shall return.) But we can say that it is what resists expression by any *customary* linguistic means; and, more particularly and more pertinently, we can say that it is what resists expression by means of the affirmation of truths.

What Derrida is drawing attention to, then, is something that can never be the subject of any truth. It is that which in some quasi-Kantian way makes possible and precedes the affirmation of any truth. There are clear links here with what each of Frege and Wittgenstein is doing. The way Derrida himself puts it is as follows. Having devised the neologism '*différance*' (with an 'a'), he writes, '*Différance* is' – where the 'is' is crossed out – 'what makes possible the presentation of the being-present.'[13] It is itself never present. This is not because it has some kind of super-being, in the way in which God might have, which means that it transcends all the finite categories in terms of which it could be made present, still less because it is straightforwardly absent. 'It exceeds the order of truth at a certain precise point,' Derrida writes, 'but without dissimulating itself as something, as a mysterious being, in the occult of a nonknowledge or in a hole with indeterminate borders (for example, in a topology of castration).'[14] *Différance* is not. It is never present; it can never be presented. Yet somehow, 'as rigorously as possible we must permit to appear/disappear the trace of what exceeds the truth of Being. The trace (of that) which can never be presented, the trace which itself can never be presented . . . '[15] It is to this end indeed that he coins the word '*différance*', whose inaudible difference from '*différence*' (with an 'e') holds it in graphic suspense between the concepts of differing and deferring, between the appearance and the disappearance of this non-presentable trace. But '*différance*' must not be understood as a name of something. Here again is Derrida:

> *Différance* has no name in our language. But we 'already know' that if it is unnameable, it is not provisionally so, not because our language has not yet found or received this *name*, or because we would have to seek it in another language, outside the finite system of our own. It is rather because there is no *name* for it at all, . . . not even [the name] of '*différance*', which is not a name . . . [16]

[13] Derrida 1982, p. 6.
[14] *Ibid.*
[15] *Ibid.*, p. 23.
[16] *Ibid.*, p. 26, emphasis in original.

Earlier in the essay he writes, '*Différance* . . . is neither a word nor a concept.'[17] Likewise Bennington, in his well known commentary, writes: 'This 'word' or 'concept' can be neither a word nor a concept, naming the condition of possibility . . . of *all* words and concepts . . . '[18] The concept of *différance* is not a concept then. Who can fail to hear the echo of Frege?

Of course, we must beware of making glib associations. It would be absurd to suggest that the very same idea has surfaced in both Derrida and Frege. But it would be just as absurd to deny that there is a common family of concerns. The interesting question, for our purposes, is whether there is a common predicament. If Frege's truck with the concept of a horse signals the failure of conceptual philosophy, does Derrida's truck with the concept of *différance* signal the failure of his style of philosophy? Anyone who is hostile to Derrida's style of philosophy will be tempted to offer it the back-handed compliment of replying, 'No. Derrida's style of philosophy is not beholden to the truth. It can tolerate falsehood and nonsense.' But perhaps this back-handed compliment can be turned into a genuine compliment: Derrida's style of philosophy (unlike conceptual philosophy) does not labour under a restricted conception of what linguistic resources are available to it; in particular, it does not treat affirmation of the truth as its sole primary mode of philosophical expression.

6.

At this point I can turn to the second of the essays by Derrida that I want to discuss, 'Signature, Event, Context'. In this essay Derrida helps us to a lively appreciation of the variety of linguistic games that can be played. Not that conceptual philosophers will be oblivious to this variety. Insofar as Wittgenstein is one of their principal mentors, how can they be?[19] Indeed one of Derrida's main concerns in this essay is to discuss certain ideas of the philosopher Austin, who certainly counts as a conceptual philosopher, and who is particularly known for his work on the different ways in which words can be used.[20] Derrida's complaint is that Austin's

---

[17] *Ibid.*, p. 7.

[18] Geoffrey Bennington, 'Derridabase', in Geoffrey Bennington and Jacques Derrida, *Jacques Derrida* (Chicago: The University of Chicago Press, 1993), pp. 73–4, emphasis in original.

[19] This question alludes primarily to Wittgenstein's later work: see e.g. *Philosophical Investigations*, §§23–4. But see also *Tractatus Logico-Philosophicus*, 4.002.

[20] See esp. J.L. Austin, *How to do Things With Words*, eds J.O. Urmson and Marina Sbisà (Oxford: Oxford University Press, 1975).

conception of language games is over-sanitized and thus unduly restrictive. He (Austin) writes as if we can cleanly separate the contexts in which it is possible to play any given language game from those in which it is not. In any other than the 'right' contexts there can at most be, on Austin's view, secondary or parasitic uses of the vocabulary associated with the game. This suggests, by extension and analogy, that we can cleanly separate the contexts in which it is possible to use any given word – with its (standard) meaning – from those in which it is not. Derrida, by contrast, urges a much more fluid understanding of the relationship between how words are used and how they mean what they do. For a word to have a meaning, it must be capable of being used in *any* context in a way that depends on, and at the same time extends, that meaning. Its meaning *is* its infinite potential for iterability in new contexts, to new effects, for new purposes, in playing new games. It would be an abrogation of a word's meaning to try to circumscribe in advance the contexts that could or could not tolerate its application, the contributions that it could or could not make to the playing of different language games. We might try to rule out a word's use in certain *linguistic* contexts, as being in violation of its meaning. For instance, we might dismiss a certain combination of words as gibberish. But even in doing this, we would be belying our purpose. For precisely in saying that the combination of words was gibberish, we would be using the word in the supposedly forbidden context. True, we would be quoting it. But it would be begging the question against Derrida to insist that our use of the word did not therefore count; that it was somehow secondary. As Derrida himself puts it,

> every sign . . . can be *cited*, put between quotation marks; thereby it can break with every given context, and engender infinitely new contexts in an absolutely nonsaturable fashion . . . This citationality, duplication, or duplicity, this iterability of the mark is not an accident or an anomaly, but is that (normal/abnormal) without which a mark could no longer even have a so-called 'normal' functioning.[21]

There are indefinitely many ways in which words can be used, then, apart from in the 'communication of presences'[22] or in the 'affirmation of truths'. There are even undemanding criteria for

---

[21]   'Signature, Event, Context', pp. 320–1, emphasis in original. Cf. p. 325.
[22]   This phrase occurs in *ibid.*, p. 316.

what makes sense whereby some uses of words count *both* as failing to make sense *and* as being utterly straightforward examples of how the words can be put to successful use in accord with their meanings. Think, for instance, of an ungrammatical string of words such as 'hungrily eat bread cheese', whose use, in a poem maybe, might – because of what the words mean – conjure up all sorts of images and have all sorts of associations and connotations and thereby convey all sorts of ideas.[23] Indeed *any* criteria for what makes sense will allow for this (that is, for the possibility of uses of words that fail to make sense even though they are in straightforward accord with the words' meanings), provided only that the criteria are not so undemanding that each use of a word that works its meaning to some effect automatically counts as making sense. Nor must we equate the nonsensical with the 'non-serious'. There is a perfectly respectable view of mathematics, for instance, according to which mathematics consists in the manipulation of nonsensical symbols: what gives the manipulation its point is its application to other uses of words, notably in science, that are not nonsensical. Derrida mentions this view in his essay, in connection with Husserl.[24] It is also, interestingly, the view that Wittgenstein endorses in his *Tractatus*, the very work in which he acknowledges what he himself has written as nonsense.[25]

Why then should there not be certain playful uses of language, perhaps involving language games in what might antecedently have been thought of as 'unsuitable' contexts, perhaps involving neologisms, perhaps involving contradictions, perhaps involving nonsense, whose effect, given the meanings of the words in play, is, if only as a matter of brute psychological fact, that those who encounter these uses, or some of those who encounter these uses, have insights that are, in some perfectly orthodox sense, ineffable? And why should philosophy not include such uses? Cannot much of Derrida's essay 'Différance' be viewed in this way? Or of Wittgenstein's *Tractatus*? – the difference perhaps being that the nonsense in the *Tractatus* masquerades as sense, thereby giving Wittgenstein's work a disingenuousness that Derrida's essay, with its overt playfulness, lacks. If so, then we are again brought to see the failure, or at least the limitations, of conceptual philosophy. Because of its commitment to a certain paradigm of language use,

[23] Cf. *ibid.*, p. 319.
[24] *Ibid.*, p. 319.
[25] *Tractatus Logico-Philosophicus*, 6.2–6.211.

namely that in which truths are affirmed, it cuts itself off from the very uses of language that are appropriate to so much that is of philosophical importance. (Who knows but that Frege would have done better if he had written 'the concept horse' under erasure?)[26]

7.

But despite the power of this onslaught, I am convinced that conceptual philosophy can withstand it. I agree that some things are ineffable. I agree that philosophy, and in particular conceptual philosophy, has to reckon with these things. And I agree that certain playful uses of language, most notably those involving the creative use of what is strictly nonsense, can be used to 'communicate' some of these things (in a sense that is quite compatible with their ineffability). These are all claims that I have been at pains to defend elsewhere.[27] But I also still want to insist that conceptual philosophy must in some sense eschew these playful uses of language; and that its own primary mode of expression is the affirmation of truths. The question is how to resolve the apparent tension between these beliefs. In attempting to answer this question, and thereby to defend conceptual philosophy, I hope not only to maintain the dialogue with Derrida but also to suggest ways in which his style of philosophy and conceptual philosophy – the style of philosophy that I try to practise myself – can be of mutual benefit.

8.

The first task confronting any conceptual philosopher trying to come to terms with the ineffable is to show how it is possible to affirm truths about the ineffable without belying its very ineffability. For example, consider my claim, earlier, that 'what Derrida is drawing attention to is something that can never be the subject of any truth'. Whatever else it was, that claim cannot have been a truth. Otherwise 'what Derrida is drawing attention to' would have been the subject of at least one truth, namely *that* one. Whenever we try to discuss the ineffable, there is a constant threat of self-stultification.

---

[26] See e.g. the translator's preface to *Of Grammatology*, pp. xiii–xx.

[27] A.W. Moore, *Points of View* (Oxford: Oxford University Press), esp. Chs. 7–9. Much of what follows in this essay is a summary of the argument of these three chapters.

A second task for any conceptual philosopher who accepts that some things are ineffable is to say what the term 'things' ranges over in this claim. If it ranges too widely, the claim is utterly trivial: you cannot put a chair into words for example. On the other hand, the most obvious way of restricting its range, namely by saying that it ranges over truths, renders the claim incoherent: 'ineffable truth' is a contradiction in terms. (Or so I would argue.)

The only decent way that I can see of discharging either task is to say that the term 'things' ranges over objects of knowledge. The claim that some things are ineffable is to be understood as the claim that some states of knowledge cannot be put into words, or more strictly, that some states of knowledge do not have any content (and therefore do not share any content with any truth). The knowledge in question is not knowledge that anything is the case. It is knowledge how to do certain things.[28] Indeed a central instance, it seems to me, is knowledge of the very kind that conceptual philosophy pursues: knowledge how to handle concepts. (This is why I think that there is a sense in which conceptual philosophy pursues knowledge but does not pursue truth.) The threat of self-stultification is annulled because there is nothing self-stultifying about discussing somebody's ineffable knowledge how to do something. We can even put into words what is involved in the person's having the knowledge. What we cannot put into words is what the person knows.

Moreover, on this construal, there is no mystery in the idea of somebody's 'communicating' something ineffable. All that is required for this to happen is that the person exploits language – plays with language – in such a way that other people come to share some of his or her ineffable knowledge. And if this does happen, or even if it could happen, then there is a way for us to reckon with the ineffable knowledge in question *without* surrendering any commitment to the truth. For we can describe the processes whereby this playful use of language, which we are at perfect liberty to talk *about*, can issue in this knowledge, which we are also at liberty to talk about, without at any point doing anything other than affirming truths.

---

[28] Or at least, it *may* be that, and very often is that. This qualification is needed to square with the answer that I gave to Thomas Baldwin during the question-and-answer session at the conference. See the transcript below.

9.

But wait! This defence of conceptual philosophy depends crucially on a distinction: the distinction between talking about playful uses of language and actually indulging in them; between adverting to 'abnormal' ways of using words and using those same words in 'abnormal' ways. Yet is this not just the kind of distinction that Derrida calls into question in 'Signature, Event, Context'?

There is a more general distinction at stake here, a distinction that many conceptual philosophers would regard as a basic analytic tool. This is the distinction between 'using' a word and 'mentioning' it: the 'use/mention' distinction.[29] A fairly orthodox way of characterizing this distinction would be as follows. Using a word involves putting it to service in a way that exploits whatever meaning it has, in order to draw attention to some aspect of reality. Mentioning a word involves putting it to service in a way that waives whatever meaning it has, in order to draw attention to the word itself. Among the various means of mentioning a word, the commonest, at least in writing, is to put the word between quotation marks. (An analogue sometimes encountered in speech is to dance one's fingers while saying the word.) Thus, by way of illustration, whereas cats have four legs, 'cats' – note the singular verb coming up – has four letters. A word that is mentioned need not itself have any sense. Thus we can say, truly, that 'splonk' has six letters. Indeed we can say, truly, that 'splonk' is a piece of nonsense. (Mentioning nonsense does not entail talking nonsense.)

It is clear how this distinction, if it were viable, could sustain any pretensions we might have to discuss certain word games while remaining faithful to the methodological principles of conceptual philosophy, and in particular while maintaining a suitable distance from playing such games ourselves: we could do this precisely by mentioning the words in play. But it is clear also that there is much in this characterization of the distinction that would be an anathema to Derrida. He once said, 'I try to place myself at a certain point at which . . . the thing signified is no longer easily separable from the signifier.'[30] And in 'Signature,

---

[29] This is one of the distinctions that J.R. Searle, in his commentary on 'Signature, Event, Context' – 'Reiterating the Differences: A Reply to Derrida', in *Glyph* 1 (1977) – famously accuses Derrida of failing to heed: see p. 203.

[30] See David Wood and Robert Bernasconi (eds.), *Derrida and 'Différance'* (Evanston: Northwestern University Press, 1988), p. 88.

Event, Context', as we have seen, he resists the idea that putting a word between quotation marks is fundamentally different from, or even 'secondary' to, doing what an advocate of the use/mention distinction would count as using the word.[31] Once Derrida's strictures have been duly taken into account, the defence of conceptual philosophy mounted above looks distinctly uneasy.

10.

I am in fact with Derrida in recoiling from much in this characterization of the use/mention distinction. It (that is to say, the characterization) does not yield the clean grammatical distinction between two ways of implementing words, each with its own clear imprint, which I take the use/mention distinction to be. However – and this is a point on which I think Derrida would agree[32] – it does not follow that there *is* no such a distinction. There is. Indeed it is a distinction with extremely important theoretical work to do. One of the greatest intellectual achievements of the twentieth century, namely Gödel's proof that arithmetic cannot be consistently and completely axiomatized, would not have been possible without due appreciation of it.[33] My

---

[31] In Jacques Derrida, *The Post Card: From Socrates to Freud and Beyond*, trans. Alan Bass (Chicago: The University of Chicago Press, 1987), pp. 97ff., he alludes, very amusingly, to the obsession that some philosophers have with the use/mention distinction, and he gently mocks their convoluted efforts to keep it clearly in focus. He writes, 'This is the problem of "'Fido'-Fido" . . . the question of knowing whether I am calling my dog or if I am mentioning the name of which he is the bearer, if I am utilizing or if I am naming his name.' He goes on, 'I adore these theorizations, often Oxonian moreover, their extraordinary and necessary subtlety as much as their imperturbable ingenuity . . . ' (p. 98). He cites an example of the tortured prose that philosophers produce when trying to respect the distinction (p. 99). And, as any student of analytic philosophy knows, there are countless other examples that he could have cited. See e.g. W.V. Quine, *Mathematical Logic* (Cambridge: Harvard University Press, 1947), §§4–6, and George Boolos, 'Quotational Ambiguity', in Paolo Leonardi and Marco Santambrogio (eds), *On Quine: New Essays* (Cambridge: Cambridge University Press, 1995).

[32] See e.g. his reply to the piece by Searle cited in note 29 above – 'Limited Inc a b c . . . ', trans. S. Weber and reprinted in his *Limited Inc*, ed. G. Graff (Evanston: Northwestern University Press, 1988) – where on p. 81 he writes, 'I agree that [the confusion of "use" and "mention"] might very well be [a radical evil].'

[33] Kurt Gödel, 'On Formally Undecidable Propositions of *Principia Mathematica* and Related Systems I', trans. Jean van Heijenoort, in Jean van Heijenoort (ed.), *From Frege to Gödel: A Source Book in Mathematical Logic, 1879–1931* (Cambridge: Harvard University Press, 1967), e.g. p. 601. See also W.V. Quine, 'Gödel's Theorem', in his *Quiddities: An Intermittently Philosophical Dictionary* (Harmondsworth: Penguin, 1990), p. 84. Actually, I think we can add that one of the great achievements, in turn, of conceptual philosophy,

opposition is not to the distinction then. It is specifically to this characterization of it.

There is not scope for me to say in detail how I think the distinction *should* be characterized. But I do insist that it is a grammatical distinction. Thus although it is true that mentioning a word involves employing it in such a way as to refer to some aspect of this very employment, the notion of reference here is a formal semantic notion tied to grammar. This is reflected in the fact that there is a range of conventional devices for mentioning a word. (Putting the word between quotation marks is indeed one of these.)

Of the various problems with the characterization above, I want to fasten on three. First, whether one is mentioning a word is *not* a question of what one is drawing attention to. What one is drawing attention to, on any given occasion by means of any given word, is a messy, complex, indeterminate matter that depends in all sorts of ways on the particular circumstances. It certainly does not just depend on the grammar of what one has said. Nor can we formulate general criteria for it which (as in the characterization above) concern the meanings of words in abstraction from their iteration in new contexts. This is precisely one of the lessons of 'Signature, Event, Context'.

The second problem is related to this. Whereas the distinction between using a word and mentioning it is a distinction of kind, the two definientia in the characterization above – exploiting a word's meaning in order to draw attention to some aspect of reality, and waiving its meaning in order to draw attention to the word itself – merge imperceptibly into each other and generate a distinction of degree. Suppose, for instance, that I assert the following:

> Albert, who remembers virtually nothing of the physics he once knew, does remember that electrons have negative charge.

Which of these two things have I just done with the word 'negative'? Or suppose I say:

> In a certain sense of 'love', it is impossible to love more than one other person.

Which of these two things have I just done with the word 'love' –

or perhaps of analytic philosophy, is to have made due appreciation of the distinction possible. Even the most rigorous writings in mathematics often flout it. See W.V. Quine, 'Use Versus Mention', in *ibid.*, p. 232.

in its first occurrence? in its second?[34] It is worth recalling in this connection Barthes' observation that all texts are 'quotations without quotation marks',[35] or the related claim that Putnam makes:

> Using any word…involves one in a history, a tradition of observation, generalization, practice and theory. – It also involves one in the activity of *interpreting* that tradition, and of adapting it to new contexts, extending and criticizing it.[36]

The third of the problems on which I wish to fasten is contextual. Even if the characterization above had been correct, it would not have helped with my defence of conceptual philosophy. If mentioning words really did involve putting them to service in a way that waived whatever meaning they had, so as to draw attention to the words themselves, then a good translation of a text in which certain words were mentioned would, all else being equal, leave those words intact. Yet clearly, if I describe, in English, the relationship between some given state of ineffable knowledge and some given playful use of language, then any examples of that use of language that I give will themselves be in English; and any translation of what I say into French will involve their French equivalents. This means that, on the characterization above, I shall not have mentioned the words in play. But mentioning the words in play was precisely what was supposed to enable me to describe that use of language while keeping a suitable distance from it.

So how does my defence of conceptual philosophy stand now?

11.

Well, ironically, I think it is bolstered. Whether one has said something that is a candidate for being true – whether one has to that

---

[34] For an expansion of these ideas see A.W. Moore, 'How Significant is the Use/Mention Distinction?', in *Analysis* 46 (1986). (But note that I do not take the same forthright attitude in that article to how the distinction should be construed. Rather I concede that there are alternative ways of construing it, and, in particular, that it can be construed as a distinction of degree. This is not the *volte-face* that it appears to be. It is just that I have elected, in the current essay, *not* to construe the distinction in one of these other ways. I could just as well have done so. But if I had, then even though much of what I have said above and much of what I shall say below would have had to be reformulated, the substance would not have been affected.)

[35] Roland Barthes, 'From Work to Text', in J.V. Harari (ed.), *Textual Strategies: Perspectives in Post-Structural Criticism* (Oxford: Methuen, 1980), p. 77.

[36] Hilary Putnam, *Reason, Truth and History* (Cambridge: Cambridge University Press, 1981), p. 203, emphasis in original.

extent conformed to the methodological paradigm of conceptual philosophy – is itself largely a matter of grammar.[37] Mentioning words, and in that quasi-technical sense talking about them, does enable us to engage with playful uses of language from a suitable distance. But precisely because it does not determine what we are drawing attention to, nor, more generally, what effect we are achieving, it also leaves us free, with due skill and artistry, to accomplish much of what can be accomplished by the very uses of language with which we are dealing, and in particular to reckon with certain philosophically important ineffable insights. Thus one thing we can do is to specify a particular ineffable insight by mentioning the nonsense that one would come out with, or the nonsense that it would in some sense be 'appropriate' to come out with, if one attempted, unsuccessfully of course, to put the insight into words. Devising such nonsense will itself involve the skill and artistry to which I have just alluded. It will involve juxtaposing words in such a way that, when their meanings are played off against one another, and against the context, this excites the insight in question. Moreover, if we did do something like this, there would be nothing fundamentally out of the ordinary about what we were doing. *Any* use of language involves *some* such skill and artistry. Putting words to service is always an imaginative exercise in which the infinite possibilities of the words' meanings are played off against one another and against the context, in order to secure some effect. Or perhaps – *perhaps* – we should except certain atypical uses of words from this claim, for example saying 'Cheese' when having one's photograph taken or writing one's name in order to test a new ballpoint (though it is unclear that *Derrida* would want to except these). But at any rate, talking about word games in such a way as to exploit whatever would be achieved in actually indulging in those games should not be excepted. Conceptual philosophers can, I think, have their cake and eat it.

The upshot of my discussion, therefore, is that there is scope for a curious and unexpected convergence of Derrida's style of philosophy with what I have been calling conceptual philosophy. What I hope to have done in this essay is to give some indication of how it is possible, first, to appropriate resources highlighted in 'Signature, Event, Context', in order, second, to reckon with inef-

---

[37] But not exclusively. For an excellent discussion see Crispin Wright, *Truth and Objectivity* (Cambridge: Harvard University Press, 1992).

fable insights afforded by 'Différance', while managing at the same time, third, to conform to methodological paradigms of conceptual philosophy. In various senses of the phrase, then – and here I echo Bennington's excellent paper[38] – this has been an attempt to 'argue with Derrida'.[39]

DISCUSSION

Jonathan Dancy: Thank you Adrian. We seem to have extra time for questions for this session. So who would like to go first?

Questioner 1: I wonder whether the paper moved a bit too quickly from the results or conclusions that Derrida sums up in such words as 'iterability' and '*différance*' to the idea of ineffability that you deployed. You suggested that in the first instance we might regard '*différance*' as marking a problem in the way that Frege thought he had marked a problem with his use of the word 'concept'. But then you tried to show that '*différance*' had something more like a positive sense – an insight connected to ineffability. So it did more than simply mark a problem. But it has been argued within other schools in the Continental field that we should only see notions such as '*différance*' as marking knotty *aporias* that one gets into with *certain* ways of thinking about things, and therefore as simply a demand to think about 'concept' and 'object' and 'reference' (which are, as it were, the 'lowest common denominators' here) in rather different ways. And one might then look to, say, Heidegger or Adorno or Wittgenstein for ways of thinking about them which are not so paradoxical.

I would also like to make a quick point about the way you talked about conceptual philosophy, as if this could be identified with analytical philosophy. You seem to exclude any kind of *explicit* metaphysics from analytical philosophy, which is not the case.

A.W. Moore: If I could perhaps just begin by commenting on the second of your two points: I am in fact prepared to recognize differences between conceptual philosophy and analytic philosophy. When Simon Glendinning encouraged me to delete the phrase 'analytic philosophy' from the paper, it wasn't simply – it

---

[38] Geoffrey Bennington, 'For the Sake of Argument (Up to a Point)', above.
[39] I am extremely grateful to Susan Durber and especially Simon Glendinning for their help in the writing of this essay.

was *almost*, but it wasn't simply! – a matter of going through it changing 'analytic philosophy', every time it occurred, to 'conceptual philosophy'. I did in fact find myself re-working various parts of the paper precisely for the reason that I think there is a difference between the two. And I entirely accept your point about ways in which analytic philosophy embraces more than what I was calling conceptual philosophy. (Indeed there may be a lack of fit in the other direction as well. That is, there may be things that deserve to be called conceptual philosophy that don't count as analytic philosophy.) I think that conceptual philosophy is a *staple* of analytic philosophy. But I think that analytic philosophy can also include conceptual innovation, designed to meet various theoretical and/or practical needs. That is, I think analytic philosophy can include the creation of concepts as well as the analysis of concepts, in a way that brings it under the umbrella of 'metaphysics'. (This is something else, incidentally, that I try to practise myself. Despite all the unwelcome connotations that the phrase has, I would be prepared to call myself an 'analytic philosopher', as much as a 'conceptual philosopher'.)

As regards your first question, I confess that I'm not absolutely sure that I've grasped it. You said that I perhaps moved a bit too quickly from talk about '*différance*', as it arises in Derrida's work, to the idea of ineffability. And I took it from the way in which your question proceeded that the idea was that I was perhaps too quickly bracketing the kind of thing that is going on in Derrida with the kind of thing that is going on in Frege. Was that the force of the question or not?

Questioner 1: Not quite! I think it makes sense as a reading of Derrida's work on '*différance*' to treat it as marking something like some kind of ineffability. Derrida suggests as much himself. I was questioning whether that was the right response to the problems that those notions show up. I was saying that I think you *should* treat it as more of a negative result, or you need an argument why that marks something we can call some sort of 'ineffability', rather than just a conceptual breakdown which we might be led through by those other philosophers I mentioned.

A.W. Moore: I may still have misunderstood the question. But I suppose ultimately the proof of the pudding is in the eating. If you think you have a problem, then whether or not your purported solution works is going to depend on what your purported solution is. You simply have to present it to people and say, 'Look, here's what I am offering. Tell me whether you think this works or not.' And I certainly didn't do anything like enough, in this paper, to show that the kind of approach to ineffability that I was championing does work. It would need to be spelled out in much more detail, with lots and lots of examples. Ultimately one would want to relate those examples to the kind of thing that is going on in the work of Derrida to see whether it really did match with his concerns and interests and with his way of doing philosophy. If it did, then that would presumably vindicate making the links between '*différance*' and ineffability that both Derrida and I want to make. It would vindicate saying various positive things using this term '*différance*', rather than just seeing the term as negatively marking a problem in the way that you suggest.

But if the links were *not* there to be made, or more pertinently, if it transpired that, at the end of the day, even using these conceptual techniques and resources, there were still things we couldn't come to terms with, couldn't cope with, and that those things were part of what was going on in Derrida's concept of '*différance*', then so be it: that would be further indication of how rich the work of Derrida is, and perhaps further indication of the need for a style of philosophy other than conceptual philosophy, to achieve something that conceptual philosophy can't achieve. It was no part of my claim, never intended to be any part of my claim, that, as it were, conceptual philosophy can do everything that needs to be done in this area and more besides. What I was trying to argue in the paper was that at any rate there wasn't internal pressure on conceptual philosophy coming from its own scrape with ineffability. Conceptual philosophy has the resources to come to terms with problems of ineffability that arise within its own domain, and indeed to come to terms with much of what people think it can't cope with that is philosophically important – but perhaps not everything.

Questioner 2: I wasn't clear about your definition of truth and what it would displace. You read Derrida as wanting to differentiate between knowledge and truth, and that led you on to defining the ineffable (which you see as the same in Derrida as in Wittgenstein) in terms of the failure or impossibility of stating the truth about the unity of language and reality. And I guess what I am quite curious about is: What is your definition of truth?

A.W. Moore: I haven't got one! If I had I would probably be much wealthier than I am and living in the States! There were all sorts of things that I was taking for granted in the paper, and one of those was the concept of truth. There are various things that I would want to say about it, but I think they would all fall short of a definition. I am thinking of truth for these purposes in a rather low-key, broadly speaking grammatical, way; by which I mean I am tying the concept of truth to the notion of a declarative sentence (which I take to be, basically, a grammatical category). So there is nothing metaphysically very ambitious about the concept of truth itself, although there might be metaphysically ambitious things involved in what you can do with the concept and how it relates to other concepts and problems in philosophy.

But it does give me the wherewithal to indicate quite sharply what I mean by ineffability, and this relates to the second part of your question. As I tried to explain in the paper, I see ineffability as a feature of certain states of knowledge. I think that the distinction between the effable and the ineffable is best drawn as a distinction between states of knowledge. And an ineffable state of knowledge is one that cannot be expressed by means of a truth. It doesn't have content; if you like, it doesn't share content with any truth – where what a truth is, for these purposes, is just a declarative sentence, or a particular application of a declarative sentence, which is true rather than false. So that is how the concept of truth is meant to connect with the concept of ineffability. (Which means, incidentally, that I *don't* define the ineffable in terms of the impossibility of stating this or that truth, as you suggested. When someone has ineffable knowledge, there's no truth there to be stated.) The concept of truth itself remains undefined for me. It remains a primitive concept about which there are various things I would like to say (and about which I wish I could say far more), but it is being put to service in this context to help to underpin the notion of ineffability which is being defined in terms of it.

Questioner 3: I am worried by what your idea of style might be. There are phrases you use which suggest that Derrida 'has a style' which could also be taken to imply that you, for example, do *not* have a style. That's the first question. Second, does not the concept of style itself tend to suggest a contingency, something extrinsic which later befalls a truth or a discourse?

A.W. Moore: In response to your first question: the implication is certainly not intended. And in fact, the very first thing on the handout is a claim about the style of philosophy of which I take myself to be an exponent.[40] So I certainly don't intend the phrase

---

[40] At the conference I distributed a handout with an outline of my argument. The first

'style' in any pejorative sense; definitely not that. Neither am I meaning to suggest that there is a way of doing philosophy which has a style in contrast to another way which is somehow free of any style. Having said that, I think that the differences that we have been talking about today, concerning various ways of doing philosophy, are, indeed, differences of style in some fairly profound sense. So I am perfectly happy to admit that I too have a style, or that the kind of philosophy that I try to do has a style.

I've forgotten the second question. But I'm not sure I followed it anyway, so could I ask you to repeat it?

Questioner 3: Yes. The danger it seems to me with the concept of style in its classical form is that it suggests something which happens later to a body of material, something which, in Derrida's terms, 'befalls' the truth or happens as a contingency after it, rather than as a necessary possibility.

A.W. Moore: I see. Well, suffice to say that that's also an implication that I don't mean to be there. Insofar as the word 'style' does have those connotations or implications, then I would want to dissociate myself from them. And that goes back to what I was saying in response to your first question: the sense in which these are styles of philosophy is a deep sense. It is not a matter of icing on the cake; not a matter of how you dress up something that could be presented with some completely different kind of dressing.

Thomas Baldwin: I want to go back to ineffability again. I'm still not clear about the connection you make between ineffability and the 'know-how/know-that' distinction. If we are thinking of Ryle's discussions, then 'know-how', in contrast to 'know-that', is strongly connected to abilities. 'Ineffability', though, was supposed to relate to an insight characteristic, perhaps, of a certain style of philosophy – of talking about '*différance*', for example. Now, is it your thought that that form of philosophy has a kind of know-how that we can't articulate as know-that? In your paper you moved a bit quickly: we had the ineffable, then we had know-how, and then we had a resolution of a problem for 'conceptual philosophy' in which we recognize that we can say true things about people's abilities. But it is not clear that that does justice to the other position. So I wonder if you could say a little more about that?

sentence on the handout was taken directly from my paper. It read: 'The style of philosophy of which I take myself to be an exponent has as its principal aim clarity of understanding and as its principal methodological tool the analysis of concepts.'

A.W. Moore: Sorry, what do you mean by 'the other position'?

Thomas Baldwin: Well, I mean someone who, like Derrida, is presenting a style of philosophy in which they are not straightforwardly putting forward truths, and who may not be all that happy about having their way of doing philosophy represented just as a kind of ability about which you, the 'conceptual philosopher', can then state some truths. For example, they find themselves, somehow, just put in the same box as people who know what it is like to be a bat!

A.W. Moore: First of all, let me say something about the connection between, on the one hand, the distinction between effable knowledge and ineffable knowledge and, on the other hand, the distinction between 'knowledge that' and 'knowledge how'. I did relate them in the paper, and I related them far too quickly, that's for sure. I certainly didn't mean to suggest that those two distinctions coincide with each other; definitely not. In particular – I can't argue for this now, because it would take a lot of arguing – I think that most standard examples of 'knowledge how', such as knowledge how to play a violin or knowledge how to ride a bike, are examples of effable knowledge, not ineffable knowledge. What I do think is that ineffable knowledge is very often – I'm not sure that I would be prepared to go as far as to say always – characterizable as 'knowledge how'. There is some 'knowledge how' which is ineffable, and possibly ineffable knowledge is always 'knowledge how', but at the very least I'm prepared to say that we can *often* characterize ineffable knowledge as 'knowledge how'.

Now, you then say, 'But doesn't this rather diminish or demean the kind of achievement that a philosopher like Derrida has made, because now it looks as if we are just equating what is going on in those texts with rather mundane exercises of practical skills?' There are various things I would want to say in response to that. I don't think, for example, that it in any sense diminishes our appreciation of a great musician, when we are sitting there listening to them playing in the concert hall, to think, 'Well, we could categorize this as "knowledge how"'. The exercise of skill that is going on in Derrida's style of philosophy still needs to go on. The kind of thing that he is doing still needs to be done, and it can be done more or less successfully. Indeed, there are plenty of examples, I think, of its being done unsuccessfully (not, I should hasten to add, by Derrida himself!). So if what is betrayed, when Derrida puts the term '*différance*' to various kinds of effect, is 'knowledge how', and if we, as conceptual philosophers, feel that we have some kind of conceptual handle on that which allows us to operate in the same territory, then I don't think this poses any threat to what he has done, or in any sense detracts from its significance. It can still seem the achievement that it originally seemed.

Jonathan Dancy: I would like to carry on with this line of questioning. I could put my worry like this. If the sort of understanding we acquire when we begin to get an understanding of '*différance*' – which you called an insight – cannot be an understanding of anything that is true (because it is ineffable), it must therefore be knowledge-how, if it is to be knowledge at all. But then the challenge is: what sort of knowledge-how is it that someone gaining that insight acquires? It looks as if such a person is acquiring something like a picture. But, surely, getting something like that picture, though, of course, to get it involves various capacities and abilities, is not *itself* a case of 'acquiring a capacity'.

A.W. Moore: You've raised a question about the ineffable knowledge associated with the word '*différance*'. But I think there is a more general question about ineffable knowledge at stake here: how such knowledge is to be characterized independently of whatever creative use of language, or nonsense, might be able to convey it. And in response to this more general question I would say: there are cases and cases. We should resist any crude generalizations at this point. I do think, as I said, that in many cases where a creative use of language can convey an ineffable insight, the way in which we would want to describe somebody who acquired such an insight would be as knowing how to do something (though incidentally, I disagree with your suggestion that, if they had knowledge which was not 'knowledge that', then it would *have* to be 'knowledge how': I don't think these categories are exhaustive within the domain of knowledge[41]). In many of these cases, as I say, we would want to describe the person as knowing how to do something. Now you say, 'Yes, but knowing how to do what?' And I would want to say, 'Very different things in the different cases.' We would need to look at the cases on a piecemeal basis. Quite often, and specifically in the case of the knowledge associated with the use of the word '*différance*', I think what we would be talking about would be knowledge how to

---

[41] See further my *Points of View* (Oxford: Oxford University Press, 1997), Ch. 8, esp. pp. 171–2.

handle concepts (knowledge of what it is for concepts to apply), or knowledge, if you like, of how to apply pictures. (You talked in terms of acquiring pictures, and perhaps pictures in this context play a similar sort of rôle to concepts.) But I certainly don't want to suggest that I have some pat formula about the kind of 'knowledge how' that is involved in all such cases. I think that we are talking about a wide variety of cases, and that a wide variety of different things are going on in them.

Ahmed Galoul: I would like to ask why conceptual philosophy should want to eat from the same cake as Derrida's! I mean, why are you looking to find convergence with Derrida in the first place? This is, after all, what you are trying to do in this chapter. But isn't it better for Derrida's philosophy, for '*la différence de Derrida*', to preserve another kind, a different kind, of philosophy than to try to look for the same kind? Isn't it a way of leading Derrida to suicide to tell him 'We are saying the same thing', even to tell him 'You are telling the truth', when he is trying to say 'What I am telling is not "the truth"'?

A.W. Moore: Well, it may be that that is a question for Derrida rather than for me! But as regards the question of why, as a conceptual philosopher, one might try to 'eat from the same cake as Derrida', well, because it is something that I think a conceptual philosopher can do, and I think it is philosophically important to do. There is territory here that it is philosophically important to enter into, and I think it is territory that conceptual philosophers *can* enter into. I think that conceptual philosophy can address the sorts of issues that I was trying to address in this chapter, without in any sense betraying its own methodological principles.

Whether that means that there is a problem for Derrida, as I say, that's a question for him rather than for me, although one thing that I think is important to emphasize in response to what you just said is that I am *not* suggesting that what Derrida is doing in his work, all the time, consists in the affirmation of truths – which is the kind of thing that I think characterizes conceptual philosophy. I'm not suggesting that the two styles of philosophy are 'the same', or that they are 'doing the same thing'. Rather I am suggesting that they have their own different ways of operating in the same territory. The sort of thing that Derrida does is still quite properly distinguished from the straightforward affirmation of truths. Indeed, it is further fuel to my case that we should want to, and that we should be able to, draw that distinction. For what I am suggesting conceptual philosophers can do here is precisely to affirm truths about the sort of thing that does not itself consist in the affirmation of truths.

Jonathan Dancy: I understand that Professor Derrida wants to speak for himself!

Jacques Derrida: I would just like to take advantage of this reference to the word 'suicide'. In what I am going to say maybe I will be 'at risk of committing suicide'. But first an anecdote. Back to Oxford, but after 1967. I see that Alan Montefiore is here today and he may remember this. We were discussing 'Différance' with some students in the gardens of Balliol College. And one of the students asked me (he is now teaching philosophy in the States by the way) 'Given what you are saying, why don't you commit suicide?' That was the question. I don't remember what the answer was. But here I am, and saying that, in fact, I am very happy with what Adrian is doing, very grateful to Adrian for what he has just been doing.

However, and before adding anything further, I want to raise two or three points with you, Adrian, so that I can explain the massive anxiety I felt, even while I was agreeing with a lot of things that you said. First, you said a moment ago that you 'took for granted' a certain concept of truth, one that is tied to declarative sentences. That's one area of anxiety for me. The second has to do with grammar. I'm not sure I quite understood what you meant by 'grammar'. The third, massive problem for me – and this has everything to do with what we are discussing here today – is around the words 'style' and 'philosophy'. Although I am professionally a philosopher, everything I do is *something else* than philosophy. No doubt it is *about* philosophy, but it is not simply 'philosophical' through and through. This is a huge issue, but since we are constantly referring to styles of 'philosophy' I think I had to bring it up. And 'style' too. I don't know what is meant by 'style' here. So each time reference is made to a 'style of philosophy' – for me it's obscure. I simply can't rely on this concept.

But having said this – and I will try to come back to some of these points – at the beginning of your paper, when you were defining conceptual philosophy, or analytic philosophy as conceptual philosophy, I thought: well, that's what I am doing, that's exactly what I am trying to do. So: I am an analytic philosopher – a conceptual philosopher. I say this very seriously. That's why there are no fronts. That's what complicates the picture. Because in France, and on the Continent in Europe (indeed, sometimes in England and America) there are many misunderstanding of what I am trying to do, and it's perhaps because I am not simply on the 'continental' side. Despite a number of appearances, my 'style' has something essential to do with a motivation that one also finds in analytic philosophy, in conceptual philosophy. From that point of view, then, there are no fronts here. I am, rather, on the side of conceptual philosophy. So the fact that you found some family resemblance between Frege's problematic and some of my concerns is not fortuitous. In my discussion with Searle there was a moment when I told him: 'You know, *you* are on the side of phenomenology, your requirements have more affinity with what I am criticizing in phenomenology than you think. Not only because of your reference to intentionality, but because of your reference to the origin, and your recourse to a supposed purity of an ideal concept.' So in that debate I already felt to be on this side rather than the 'continental' side.

I was also very interested and struck by what you said about knowledge and truth, and the way in which you try to dissociate knowledge and the possession of truth. I think I would want to develop this further. At one point you said that 'conceptual philosophy may not involve the pursuit of truth in the way in which science does, but there is an important sense, it seems to me, in which conceptual philosophy has a *commitment* to the truth.' Commitment to the truth. But I think I too have such a commitment to the truth – if only to question the possibility of the truth, the history of the truth, the differences in the concept of truth, and not taking for granted the definition of truth as tied to declarative sentences. Indeed, if we turn to the text of 'Différance' that you refer to, it is in the name of the truth, of a certain truth, that I say that '*différance*' is not a name nor a concept'. Of course, the truth that I am committed to in that case is not the truth of a judgment, is not truth as the adequation of a judgment, nor is it truth as the revelation of Being as such. It is something else to which one is committed. But what does that mean? What does it mean to be committed? I would be tempted to connect what you say about 'commitment to truth' with what you say about 'doing' and 'knowledge-how' to do certain things. For a commitment is not a theoretical matter, but an engagement which calls for performative gestures. However, in the case of the commitment you talk about, 'doing' is not necessarily a case of 'knowing how to do', is not only or necessarily the exercise of a skill or a talent or a technique. It is also a responsibility – a way of respecting a commitment.

With this in view, let's take the difficult example of the concept of 'decision'. Of course, being committed to something is being committed to make decisions in a certain way, to take responsibilities. Here, then, the concept of decision has nothing to do in itself with any knowledge. You make a decision because of a commitment, but through a leap *beyond* any knowledge. But, in that case, the concept of the truth, as the end of the theme of a commitment, is not the concept of a theoretical truth, neither as a true declarative sentence nor the adequation of judgment nor a revelation of Being. It is something else.

Again, what is it then? It is, for instance, the truth of someone who tells the truth in a testimony. To tell the truth in a testimony, as a witness, does not compel you to say something true. You may say something false while telling the truth – while being sincere and truthful. In that case the truth in a testimony has nothing to do with the truth in a theoretical sense. Sometimes you may speak truthfully while giving a false testimony. The concept of truth has to be re-thought in this context. Now, in the passage of 'Différance' that you quote, when I say '"*différance*" is not a name', of course grammatically it is wrong. It is a name, no doubt. But then it is not the name of an *object*, not the name of some 'being' that could be present. And for that reason it is not a concept either in the Fregean sense; that is, a concept of some*thing* – say, a concept of a horse. So when I say it is not a concept nor a name I'm not simply saying something wrong. On the contrary, I think I am saying something which is committed to some truth. But, then, what is that truth? That remains to be defined and it is in relation to that truth that some responsibility has to be taken.

So, on the one hand, you are right when you say of my remark that one can 'hear the echo of Frege'. Yes. But, on the other hand, no! Its not exactly the same when you say 'the concept of *différance* is not a concept', as when you say 'the concept of a horse is not a concept'. Indeed, since we know what a horse is (in principle), and know that it is a definite object, then in a certain way my remark is exactly the opposite to Frege's. Thus even if Frege's question is in the same family as my own, it is, at the same time, very different.

A.W. Moore: Could I just respond to that last point? I don't think it is as different as you're suggesting. The specific example that we take from Frege concerns one particular concept, the concept of a horse, whereas *différance* seems to have, apart from anything else, a generality that goes way beyond that specific example. But of course, the problem that's vexing Frege is not a problem specifically about horses. In fact, it has much more to do with the 'is' in ' . . . is a horse' than with the 'horse'. It is the very general problem of predication, which could just as well be exemplified by a predicate like ' . . . is green', or ' . . . is a house', or any other of countless examples that we could think of. It is the very idea of predication that Frege is exercised by; the very idea that parts of language can hook up with each other in such a way as to say what the world is like, rather than being a mere catalogue of names. And I think that once you think in terms of that very general linguistic problem, and the metaphysical underpinnings and echoes that it has, then Frege's concerns seem quite a lot closer to your work than the comments you just made were suggesting. I don't for one minute want to suggest – and I was explicit about this in the paper – that you and Frege are addressing exactly the same problem. But I do think that your concerns are very closely related, and perhaps more closely related than you were suggesting. Frege's problem is a problem about the copula. It is a problem about parts of language that are not themselves used to refer to objects ('things') though they are a precondition of the very possibility of our saying anything about objects; of our saying anything at all. Once we've put it like that, then the connections to your work probably seem much closer.

David Roden: My question is about the formal semantic relation of 'reference' that you alluded to earlier. If we can accept that Derrida's iterability arguments in some way complicate our notions of a semantic nature or the idea that there is some 'essence' which defines and delimits the boundaries of the use of a word, then surely that also complicates, for example, the distinction between type and token – in the sense that the type would presumably be delimited by that essence, but if there are no such essences then the distinction between type and token is itself problematic.

Now as I understand it, most of the standard accounts of quotation in the analytical literature treat it as a kind of 'reference by exemplification' so that, as Davidson says, we 'refer' to the type via an object which 'has it'. But of course if it doesn't 'have it' then we can't 'refer' to it either and if that's the case then the kind of quarantine that you are trying to enforce between, if you like, the 'ludic' object language and the metalanguage of strictly conceptual analysis seems to be somewhat shaky in the sense that the object language vacillation comes to 'infect' the metalanguage.

The very relation of reference becomes undetermined and in a sense you get a kind of *différance* at the level of the metalanguage. A.W. Moore: I think that that is an exceedingly interesting and important question, if I may say so. It is true that any account of the use/mention distinction along the lines I was suggesting would ultimately have to reckon with precisely the problems you have just put your finger on. And I must confess that here and now there isn't anything very helpful that I can say in response to you, though I can perhaps gesture in the kind of direction in which I think the account would have to go. If there really are these problems about the type/token distinction, and if, in particular, the notion of a type carries with it some unwarranted essentialism, then it's possible that we could get the kind of mileage out of the use/mention distinction that I was hoping we could get, just by operating at the level (so to speak) of tokens. (Of course, it wouldn't then be correct to *call* them tokens: what I mean are the dated utterances and inscriptions that get called tokens by those who accept the distinction.) You alluded to Davidson's work, and, as you quite rightly point out, Davidson's account of quotation, or more particularly of the use of quotation marks, is that they're used as demonstrative devices: a pair of quotation marks is used to refer to a type by demonstrating something that exemplifies it, by demonstrating a token of that type.[42] Well, if the notion of a type is problematic, and we couldn't any longer see things in those terms, then maybe what we could do would be to turn to an account of the use/mention distinction that was actually more straightforward, an account whereby the quotation marks were being used just to refer to the 'token' itself, by demonstrating that token. So in that sense, the account would just operate at the level of tokens. I suspect that a lot of the same machinery would work in that context. But I agree that this is a very important question that would need to be thought through. Dawn Phillips: When you rejected the original characterization of the use/mention distinction, you said that you thought the distinction was a grammatical one. You said that you weren't intending to go into any details, and so I'm sorry to drag you down that route, but I was just wondering if another way of characterizing it might be by looking at Wittgenstein's distinction between empirical and grammatical propositions. This would

[42] Donald Davidson, 'Quotation', reprinted in his *Inquiries into Truth and Interpretation* (Oxford: Oxford University Press, 1984).

bring in the idea of 'knowing how to go on' – the notion of the mastery of a technique for a language-game – as relating to the kind of knowledge that one has of grammatical propositions.

A.W. Moore: Actually, when I said at that point in my paper that I saw the use/mention distinction as a grammatical distinction, what I had in mind was the kind of thing I was just talking about in response to the previous question, thinking of it in terms of something like a Fregean notion of reference. In particular, I had in mind the Davidsonian approach to quotation. Now I confess I hadn't thought about how that might relate to Wittgenstein's distinction between grammatical propositions and empirical propositions, and offhand I still don't see an obvious connection. What I do recognize and would want to emphasize is the second of the connections that you emphasized: the connection between grammatical propositions and the kind of practical knowledge that I was talking about as an example of ineffable knowledge. How all of that relates to the use/mention distinction is complex, and, as I say, I can't offhand see direct connections – although of course, it is part of my thesis that there are all sorts of indirect connections.

SESSION THREE

Simon Glendinning (chair): In this session I find myself in the somewhat disconcerting situation of being surrounded by participants who are all, in some way, my teachers.[1] Only some of them have been my teachers in what philosophers used to get away with calling the 'strict and literal' sense. The rest have been my teachers only through what might be called (if it did not seem so readily generalisable) 'distance learning'. Except, perhaps, for one complicated case. And that is Jacques Derrida. He is, of course, for me, 'a teacher'. (I am not sure what he has taught me: whether it is a know-how or a certain kind of pleasure.) But I hesitate to place him in line with my other teachers-at-a-distance. For what is at issue for me in his case is a deep kind of formation. Even if there are always distances, he figures as a kind of point of departure for my thinking, not just as someone who has introduced me to or helped me think (better) about other things. In this respect he stands, for me, alongside Wittgenstein and Heidegger. So I am unbelievably grateful to him for coming to this conference. It is very special for me.

And now we have some time to talk with him. This session will consist of two halves. In the first half we have Tom Baldwin, Professor of Philosophy at the University of York, who will put a series of related questions to Derrida under the title 'Death and Meaning'. That will be followed by Stephen Mulhall, Fellow of New College, Oxford, who will, in effect, be posing just a single, if rather singular, question to Derrida about Wittgenstein and deconstruction. In each case Derrida will have an opportunity to respond following the presentation. So without more ado I would like to invite Tom Baldwin to put his questions to Derrida.

DEATH AND MEANING – SOME QUESTIONS FOR DERRIDA

Thomas Baldwin

Derrida prefaces one of his early works *Speech and Phenomena* with

[1]   All the participants at the conference were at the table for this session.

a passage from one of Edgar Allan Poe's tales 'The Facts in the Case of M. Valdemar':

> I have spoken both of 'sound' and 'voice'. I mean to say that the sound was one of distinct, of even wonderfully, thrillingly distinct, syllabification. M. Valdemar *spoke*, obviously in reply to the question. . . . He now said:
> 'Yes; – no no; – I have been sleeping – and now – now – I *am dead*.' (Derrida 1973, p. 1)

An enigmatic passage (I won't take up time explaining Poe's story): why does Derrida choose it? Not just because of the emphasis on 'sound', 'voice' and speech, but also because of M. Valdemar's paradoxical affirmation of his own death: 'I am dead'. Derrida wants to indicate here, right from the start, a thesis that runs through the book, that there is a connection between meaning and death, that somehow the possibility of meaning is dependent upon the inevitability of death. I shall try to say more about what the connection is supposed to be in a moment, but let me explain first why I have picked Derrida's prefatory citation of this passage as the way of introducing my own remarks. The reason is that in thinking about the questions I wanted to put to Derrida on this occasion it struck me that in one way or another they connect with this theme of death. As I have indicated, he announces this theme at the start of *Speech and Phenomena*, the book with which he launched his critique of the metaphysics of presence, and one has only to turn to *The Gift of Death* (1995) to find him still concerned with the subject. So let me now just list, as my agenda for this occasion, the topics I want to raise through this connection:

1. Writing and *différance*
2. Others
3. Negation
4. Animals
5. The singular individual

1. Writing and *Différance*

So what was the point of citing the passage from Poe? Derrida explains as follows:

> The *Bedeutung* <meaning> 'I am' or 'I am alive'...is what it is...only if it is not impaired by falsity, that is, if I can be dead at

the moment when it is functioning... This is not an extraordinary tale by Poe but the ordinary story of language. (Derrida
1973, pp. 96–7)

That is, it is an essential feature of language that meaning does
not depend upon truth, that the possibility of falsity must be
allowed for; so what is meant by my utterances of 'I am alive'
continues to make sense even when I am dead. But this can be
true only where the meaning of the words does not depend on my
continued existence; and this, Derrida tells us, is precisely what
'writing' amounts to. It (writing) is 'the common name for signs
which function despite the total absence of the subject because of
(beyond) his death' (*ibid.*, p. 93). So the horror of Poe's story –
the story of a corpse that speaks – reminds us of 'the ordinary
story of language', that all language is (in this sense) writing. This
conception of language contrasts in Derrida's text with that which
he (a little uncharitably in my view) ascribes to Husserl, according
to which its meaning depends upon the way in which a speaker
gives life to it as a sign by breathing into it a meaning that is as
evanescent as the speaker's own experience of which the meaning
is supposed to be an expression. On this conception, the sign
'does not risk death in the body of a signifier that is given over to
the world' (*ibid.*, p.77); but, equally, because such a sign cannot
function in the absence of the subject it cannot have a meaning
at all. It is essential to language that M. Valdemar does not need
to be alive for us to be able to say of him that he is dead, thereby
saying of him what he would say were he to speak the words 'I am
dead'.

The thought that meaning can survive death connects with a
different element in Husserl's thought, which Derrida rightly
identifies as Platonist – the conception of meanings, not as
expressions of present consciousness, but, on the contrary, as
'transcendental' – in the sense that they are entirely removed
from the empirical contingencies of space and time. Derrida uses
the theme of death in his critique of this conception as well, but
I am not sure that I follow his reasoning at this point (see *ibid.*, pp.
53ff.), and my uncertainty in this area will lead me into my first
question to him. One possible line of thought here would run as
follows: this transcendental conception of meaning induces a
correlative transcendental conception of myself. For only a being
similarly freed from the contingencies of space and time could
grasp transcendental meanings of this kind; and such a being (as

Plato famously argued in the *Phaedo*) must be immortal. But we know that we are not immortal. So the Platonist conception of meaning must be rejected.

My impression, however, is that this line of thought, with its simple assertion that we just know that we are not immortal, does not do justice to Derrida's reasoning at this point and I do not altogether follow the argument at this point. But it is not important to sort out that matter here: what is of more interest is the thesis itself, that '*différance* becomes the finitude of life as an essential relation with oneself and one's death' (*ibid.*, p. 102; cf. Derrida 1974, p. 143 and p. 236).

'*Différance*' is of course Derrida's central characterization of meaning. In it he combines the familiar structuralist thesis of the holistic aspect of meaning as arising within a system of arbitrary signs with his own, distinctive affirmation that meaning involves the possibility of repetition, or, as I would say, rule-following, through which some reasonably determinate concept is characterised. Since this 'originally repetitive structure' (Derrida 1973, p. 56) of signs implies that their meaning cannot be entirely 'present' to a speaker whose practice, though regular, is 'blind' (as Wittgenstein puts it), it follows that *différance* (meaning) depends as much on what is absent as on what is present; that there is a characteristic interplay between the speaker's present intentions in speaking as he does and his use of the same words on other, now absent, occasions.

This much is, I think, clear enough and, indeed, correct. But what still puzzles me is the way in which this repetitive, regular, structure of *différance* is supposed to give rise to – or is it to depend upon? – 'the finitude of life as an essential relation with oneself and one's death' (*ibid.*, p. 102). There is here a reversal of the moral of Poe's tale. The moral there was that it is essential to meaning that it can survive death; but now we are told that it also depends upon death, that it is a phenomenon of finitude. My first question then is just why we should assent to this. I raise this question not just for its own sake, but because of its role in the context in which I first raised it, namely Derrida's rejection of Platonism, and indeed his rejection of 'metaphysics' in general. These are important themes and I should like to be clearer than I am at present as to just why Derrida ties *différance*, and thus meaning, to finitude. I shall return briefly to this question in a moment, and then again at the very end of my remarks.

2. Others

Anyone who reads Derrida having already familiarised themselves with the debates in English-language philosophy that we associate with Wittgenstein's 'Private Language Argument' is bound to be struck by the similarities between, on the one hand, Wittgenstein's critique of the possibility of private ostensive definition and, on the other, Derrida's critique of the 'myth of presence'. But then one difference must equally strike a reader; namely, that whereas Wittgenstein's argument focuses on a contrast between the private and the public, Derrida's focuses on a contrast between the present and the absent. So my second question is this: is *différance*, this 'originally repetitive structure' of language, essentially public? Is some involvement with others essentially implicated in the use of language that counts as '*différance*'?

There are suggestions in Derrida to this effect. For example he writes: 'Intersubjectivity is inseparable from temporalization taken as the openness of the present upon an outside of itself, upon another absolute present' (Derrida 1973, p. 84n). But, as this passage indicates, for him it is the 'temporalization' of meaning that carries the burden of his argument: it is the ecstatic, potentially repetitive structure of *différance* that bursts the confines of anything merely present through its essential reference to that which is not present. But is there here a distinction – between other times and other minds – without a difference? Well, if one thinks back to the Wittgensteinian debates again, it is clear that there are substantive issues, concerning the alleged normativity of meaning and the role of a community in sustaining the practice of a language-game, which involve other minds rather more than other times. Obviously I don't want here to raise all those questions directly. But it would be interesting to hear from Derrida how he now sees the priorities in this area – is the involvement of others in *différance* something essentially derivative – dependent upon the ecstatic structure of temporalisation? Or is it absolutely fundamental in a way that might connect *différance* with that Hegelian conception of self-consciousness that is utterly dependent upon involvement with others? (My own small suggestion here is that if an involvement with other minds is as fundamental as an involvement with other times, then we can use the ambiguity of the verb 'to defer' in English, between deference to others and temporal deferral, to propose that meaning thus understood is, not *différance* which draws on a different ambiguity in French that is not matched in English, but, say, 'deferance'!) And now a final note in passing to connect back with my general question of our relationship with death. For Hegel, although an involvement with others is inescapably necessary for self-consciousness, it is also the case that the paradigm of any such involvement is mortal combat: for 'the individual who has not risked his life...has not attained to the truth of this recognition as an independent self-consciousness' (Hegel 1977, p. 114). Thus for Hegel, somewhere in the shadow of all social relations there lies the fear of death. Hence, if *différance* is essentially public, or socially constituted, in a way that echoes this Hegelian dialectic, we will get to the conclusion that I was wondering about earlier, that *différance* involves 'an essential relation with one's death'. Is Derrida perhaps a Hegelian – at least in this respect?

3. Negation

For Hegel, death was a form of negation – the 'natural negation of consciousness' (Hegel 1977, p. 188). For Derrida too, *différance*, this 'essential relation with one's death', is also essentially, but always paradoxically, negative. Here are some of Derrida's characterisations, which concern not just *différance*, but also the closely related concepts of 'trace' and 'supplementarity':

> It [sc. the movement of *différance*] produces sameness as self-relation within self-difference; it produces sameness as the nonidentical. (Derrida 1973, p .82)
> It [sc. the concept of trace] is in fact contradictory and not acceptable within the logic of identity. (Derrida 1974, p. 61)
> Supplementarity, which *is nothing*, neither a presence nor an absence, is neither a substance nor an essence of man. (*ibid.*, p. 244)
> ... we designate the impossibility of formulating the movement of supplementarity within the classical logos, within the logic of identity... (*ibid.*, p. 314)

For anyone who knows their French philosophy, these phrases will have an immediate resonance: this is surely the voice of Jean-Paul Sartre. And indeed Derrida himself implicitly acknowledges as much when he observes that 'auto-affection' – which is both the characteristic self-consciousness of oneself in speaking and, he says, the movement of *différance* – is 'subjectivity or the for-itself'

(Derrida 1973, p. 79). Now I do not say that *différance* and the rest are just redescriptions of that old war-horse, the for-itself – since that is essentially tied into the metaphysics of presence, being precisely a paradoxical 'presence to itself'. Nonetheless, it is very striking to see how the Sartrean theme of the for-itself as *Le Néant* surfaces in Derrida's texts; the relationship between the for-itself and *différance* is, one might say, a case of Lamarckian evolution by inheritance of acquired features. In particular Derrida seems to have adopted one of the most problematic features of Sartre's metaphysics; namely, the thesis that the principle of 'identity' (or non-contradiction) is a principle with only a limited area of application (cf. Sartre 1958, p. 58); so that there is another area – which Sartre will call 'consciousness' and Derrida 'supplementarity' (or perhaps even grammatology itself), which can somehow evade the logic of non-contradiction.

Not surprisingly, these are claims with which I have little antecedent sympathy and patience. The limits of logic are the limits, not just of the world, but also of 'good sense' (as Derrida himself acknowledges at one point – 1988, p. 127) and contradiction is not a condition to be embraced as if it provides a mode of being superior to the mundane logic of mere common sense. Instead it is a form of intellectual dry-rot which is likely to spread and destroy the significance of any theory which admits it. But Derrida's position here is closely connected to a theme which is central to his early work, at least: that of the distinction between empirical science (including, I take it, empirical linguistics) and philosophical reflections on the conditions of the possibility of science. For he claims that *différance* is fundamental with regard to this very distinction (Derrida 1974, p. 23), and, clearly if ordinary logic is restricted in its application to empirical science, then *différance*, insofar as it a non-scientific inquiry into the possibility of science is not similarly restricted.

It is, then, this theme that forms the background to my third question, or rather, group of questions. Let me call this theme that of Derrida's 'transcendentalism'. This characterisation is, I think, appropriate despite his rejection of Husserl's Platonist conception of meaning as the 'transcendental signified'; for he himself maintains that *différance* organises empirical concepts in a 'quasi'-transcendental manner' (Derrida 1988, p. 127). My first question, then, concerns what can be said concerning *différance* if, as I have tried to suggest, its transcendental status excludes it from ordinary logic and thus good sense. English-language philosophers will again be reminded of Wittgenstein, but this time the Wittgenstein of the *Tractatus* whose philosophy condemns itself to be ultimately '*unsinnig*' (nonsense). Is that a fate for which Derrida seeks to prepare his own philosophy? But if so, then what status is one to give to his own critique of Husserl's theory of signs, or to his claim that *différance* has an 'originally repetitive structure'? That sounds like a thesis that is being put forward as true (and not, indeed, to switch to the idioms of the *Investigations*, as a thesis so banal that 'it would never be possible to debate them, because everyone would agree to them' Wittgenstein 1958, §128).

My next question here concerns Derrida's attitude to his own transcendentalism, to the merits of the distinction that he draws between empirical science and the work of *différance*. When Derrida says that 'it is impossible to have a science of the origin of presence' (Derrida 1974, p. 63) he sounds like a traditional philosopher claiming that the empirical sciences stand in need of a transcendental foundation, except that he goes on to say that this foundation is not to be found in some a priori system of reason but in the playful non-science of *différance*. Yet we can ask why Derrida continues to rely on the distinctions that he employs here – ontic/ontological, empirical/transcendental, positive science/ grammatology? etc.. Again, within English-language philosophy we have learnt to be suspicious of these distinctions and the foundationalist assumptions they seem to bring with them (here, of course, it is Quine who is the master of suspicion). For myself, I find these matters complicated in ways that I shall not try to explain; but it would be good to hear from Derrida how strongly he remains committed to the distinctions which seem to inform his work. My final question on this theme of 'transcendentalism' is perhaps a way of re-emphasizing the previous one. In his early work, when discussing Husserl, Derrida is critical of the conception of 'constituting consciousness'. He writes: 'There is no constituting subjectivity. The very concept of constitution itself must be deconstructed' (Derrida 1973, p. 85n). Yet when I turn to his work and try to think through the account of deconstruction given in such claims as this:

> One of the definitions of what is called deconstruction would be the effort to take this limitless context [sc. the entire 'real-history-of-the-world'] into account, to pay the sharpest and broadest attention possible to context, and thus to an incessant

movement of recontextualisation. The phrase which for some has become a sort of slogan, in general so badly misunderstood, of deconstruction ('there is nothing outside the text' [*il n'y a pas de hors-texte*]) means nothing else: there is nothing outside context. (Derrida 1988, p. 136)

I am led to wonder whether some work of inescapable contextual constitution is not here presupposed, not now a 'subjective' constitution but a kind of transcendental constitution located instead in the differantial play of signs. So is the play of *différance* not just a constituting consciousness which has taken the linguistic turn? Foucault famously called Sartre '*le dernier philosophe*', but I wonder if Derrida is not the last transcendental idealist?

4. Animals

After all that heavy duty philosophy, my next question is much more straightforward and concerns Derrida's attitude to the mental life of brute animals. In his early work he seems to be a sceptic:

> If we consider the *concept* of animality not in its content of understanding or misunderstanding but in its specific *function*, we shall see that it must locate a moment of *life* which knows nothing of symbol, substitution, lack and supplementary addition, etc. – everything, in fact, whose appearance and play I wish to describe here. A life that has not yet broached the play of supplementarity and which has not yet let itself be violated by it: a life without *différance* and without articulation. (Derrida 1974, p. 242)

If animal life is a life without *différance*, then it is a life without the kinds of thought that we enjoy, as speakers and writers at least. Does that imply that it is life without thought at all? Derrida does not say. But he clearly cannot allow that there is an important domain of thought that is independent of *différance*: for such a domain must also be available to us too, since we are animals as well; in which case it would radically undermine the significance of his 'grammatology', his account of language, if it turned out that some important domain of thoughts is quite unaffected by this account.

The difficulty here is familiar. On the one hand, there are theorists from Descartes onwards who associate thought and language.

On the other hand, the implication that brute animals have no mental life is unacceptable to us. Bernard Williams cites a lovely passage from a letter by Henry More to Descartes on this subject: 'But there is nothing in your opinions that so much disgusts me, so far as I have any kindness or gentleness, as the internecine and murderous view which you bring forward in the *Method*, which snatches away life and sensibility from all the animals' (Williams 1978, p. 282). Somehow there needs to be a way between Cartesian scepticism and simple-minded anthropomorphism. But because language itself does not come in degrees, it does not provide a helpful way into this matter.

In the 'Letter on Humanism' Heidegger faced the same problem as Derrida. He famously writes here that animals which lack a language are 'never placed freely in the clearing of Being which alone is "world"'(Heidegger 1993, p. 230. Heidegger's 'clearing of Being' is directly comparable to Derrida's play of *différance*). And yet Heidegger also says here that animals are not 'suspended worldlessly in their environment' (*ibid.*). But no positive account of their situation is offered. However, in his essay on Heidegger, *Of Spirit*, Derrida calls attention to an earlier, more helpful, discussion by Heidegger in his 1929/30 Freiburg lectures (published as *The Fundamental Concepts of Metaphysics*, trans. W. McNeil and N. Walker, Bloomington: Indiana University Press, 1995). Heidegger here develops at great length the thesis that what is distinctive of animals is that they are '*weltarm*' – poor in world: i.e. they do have a world but one that is radically impoverished in relation to ours in ways which Heidegger discusses with perceptive detail. I have the impression from his discussion that Derrida finds this a helpful idea, though he also stresses how subversive this line of thought threatens to become for Heidegger – since animals so conceived fall outside the categories of *Being and Time*.(Perhaps this point has something to do with the fact that Heidegger does not draw later on this long discussion of the impoverished world of animals.) However that may be, this issue provides a context (remember – 'there is nothing outside context') for my question to Derrida concerning the status of animals: has he been able to develop a way of thinking about them which does justice to our quite unforced willingness to ascribe thoughts and feelings to them without threatening the conception of *différance* elaborated in his early work?

5. The Singular Individual

It may have been noticed that I made no reference to death in my discussion of animals and the question of their being. The connection here is a bit forced – it is just that at one point, as Derrida notes, Heidegger suggests that one thing that separates animals from us is that because they lack our kind of anticipatory understanding of death, their being is not being-towards-death (Derrida 1989, pp. 119–20). Derrida does not seem to regard this as a particularly helpful suggestion, and I don't want to pursue the matter. Instead I want to turn to Derrida's discussion of being-for-death in his meditations on death, *The Gift of Death* [*Donner la mort*]. One implication of this discussion will indeed be that Heidegger's suggestion does point to a way in which animals differ profoundly from us, but, equally, that it does not cast much light on the vexed question of their mental life.

In *The Gift of Death* Derrida discusses Heidegger's conception of Being-towards-death (*Sein-zum-Tode*) and defends Heidegger's famous claims, first, that for each of us, our own death is irreplaceable ('no one can die my death for me') and, second, that it is through a sense of the ultimate irreplaceability of ourselves in death that we are led to a conception of ourselves as unique, singular, individuals. Derrida puts the point in this way: 'It is in the being-towards-death that the self of the *Jemeinigkeit* [the 'in each case mineness'] is constituted' (Derrida 1995, p. 45)

I do not want to enter into a detailed discussion of the merits of these points. Instead I want to pick up a point that Derrida himself takes from them and then uses as the basis for an extended line of thought which gives rise to my fifth and final question.

The point concerns a feature of the conception of the self that is precipitated by this Heideggerian line of thought, namely the conception of the self as 'unsubstitutable' (Derrida 1995, p. 45). The thought is roughly this. In recognising that no one can take away from me the necessity of death, I am led to recognise that there are aspects of my life for which no one else can be a substitute for me. And it is then these aspects of my life which constitute me as a 'singular individual'. Now there is then a sharp contrast between this conception of the self as an 'unsubstitutable' singular individual and Derrida's earlier conception (in *On Grammatology* at least) of the play of *différance* in which he draws explicitly upon the way in which language provides an indefinite series of 'supplements', or substitutes. Thus he remarks:

> What we have tried to show by following the guiding line of the "dangerous supplement" is . . . that there has never been anything but writing; there have never been anything but supplements, substitutive significations which could only come forth in a chain of differential references. (Derrida 1974 pp. 158–9)

Derrida has been talking here about Rousseau. Here, now, is his summary conclusion: 'What does Rousseau say without saying, see without seeing? That substitution has always already begun' (*ibid.* p. 215).

In drawing attention to this contrast I am not, I stress, trying to find fault with Derrida, to point to an inconsistency in his thought. Not surprisingly, he himself he is well aware of this contrast, and it forms the basis of his discussion in *The Gift of Death* itself of Kierkegaard's treatment of the story of Abraham and Isaac in *Fear and Trembling*. Central to this is the contrast between a domain which depends upon the possibility of substitutions and one which excludes them: because language belongs to the former, our lives as singular individuals, which belong to the latter, pass in silence – 'as soon as one speaks,…one loses that very singularity' (Derrida 1995, p. 60). Derrida develops this point in the context of Kiekegaard's discussion of Abraham: the domain of language is also the domain of the ethical, for ethical rules are inherently universal and thus belong in the domain within which substitution is permitted (one might query the association here between universality and substitutability, but I shall not pursue the matter). Abraham, however, finds himself outside this domain: God's demand that he should take his son Isaac and sacrifice him cannot be accommodated within the ethical and belongs instead to Abraham as a singular individual with a relationship of faith in his God about which he cannot speak.

For Kierkegaard this domain of the singular individual is that of religion, since for Kierkegaard one's sense of oneself as an unsubstitutable singular individual is only attained through consciousness of sin and of one's dependence upon God's grace. Derrida, as we have seen, adopts Heidegger's transformation of this schema which substitutes (!) being-towards-death for consciousness of sin. Furthermore he then opens out the conception of singularity further by adding that 'no one can make a decision . . . in my place' (Derrida 1995, p. 60); so the domain of singularity now includes those personal decisions which are irreducibly mine and mine alone. As a result Kierkegaard's contrast between ethics and religion is transformed by Derrida into a contrast between the ethical, conceived as the system of general public values (in particular justice) and that of personal decision, typically between competing and incommensurable obligations. It may be said, of course, that this is just a redescription of Kierkegaard's contrast: Derrida suggests we might think of our talk of God as a way of characterising 'a structure of conscience', the possibility for each of us of having 'a secret relationship with myself' (*ibid.*, pp. 108–9). Let us not pursue that line of thought. Nonetheless it is worth pausing to note that once Derrida's redescription of this domain of singularity has been effected we are on familiar territory. For a second time, surely, Derrida speaks here with a Sartrean voice. For who is this singular individual, compelled to take absolute responsibility for a decision that no one else can take for him? He is that young man in occupied France who has to decide, to choose, between staying to look after his mother who lacks any other means of support or leaving France to join the Free French (Sartre 1989, pp. 35–6). I do not intend this comparison as a criticism, nor should it really come as a surprise. After all Derrida is here discussing Kierkegaard and Sartre was the great French existentialist. But it does now bring me to the pair of questions with which I will end. For Sartre this sphere of personal decision is definitive of man; it is what he has in mind when he writes of 'freedom' as defining 'man' (*ibid.*, p. 34). In *Of Grammatology*, by contrast, it is precisely not this sphere of unsubstitutable singularity that is definitive of man: instead – 'supplementarity <which of course brings with it substitution> makes possible all that which is proper to man: speech, society, passion, etc.' (Derrida 1974, p. 244 – translation corrected). He also goes on to say here 'All concepts determining a non-supplementarity (nature, animality, primitivism, childhood, madness, divinity etc.) have evidently no truth-value' (*ibid.*, p. 245).

As I see it, the later work I have been discussing would lead Derrida to qualify this remark; for the sphere of individual singularity, although one of 'non-supplementarity', does not, I take it, belong with those which he here groups together as lacking a truth-value (whatever quite that means). But the question remains as to whether he would also now want to qualify also his remarks about what is proper to man, not by becoming a Sartrean existentialist (heaven forbid!) but by allowing more explicitly for a duality in human life between the spheres of supplementarity and singularity.

Last of all, now, back to the beginning, not quite all the way back to Poe, but to the thesis that I queried, that '*différance*...becomes the finitude of life as an essential relation with oneself and one's death' (Derrida 1973, p. 102). Surely, from the perspective of Derrida's later work, this claim yokes together themes that should be kept apart: *différance* goes with supplementarity and the essential possibility of substitutions, whereas 'the finitude of life as an essential relation with oneself and one's death' goes with singularity, the fact that no one else can die my death, and thus the impossibility of substitution. So perhaps my first question receives in this way an answer.

DERRIDA'S RESPONSE TO BALDWIN

Jacques Derrida: Thank you very much, Tom, for such a generous set of questions and objections. I really won't be able to respond, but I shall try to say something, as clearly and as briefly as possible.

Let me start, as you do, with the quote from Poe. If we restrict ourselves to the immediate context, then, of course, death has been a constant theme. But that doesn't mean that, in this case, death is what matters. You translate my propositions into a thesis that the possibility of meaning is dependent on the *inevitability* of death. But, what I have been talking about is the *possibility* of death. It is not a thesis on our mortality. I am not saying 'We are mortal' or 'Death is inevitable'. I would be inclined to think so! But that is not the point. The point is that for a sentence such as 'I am dead' to *be* a sentence – an intelligible, meaningful sentence – it has to be implied that I may be absent and that it can continue to function. The functioning of the sentence doesn't require my being present to it. On the contrary, the functioning of the sentence implies the possibility of my being radically 'on leave' so to speak, radically absent. So, when I speak of death in this case, it is just a figure to refer to this absence, to refer to the structural conditions of possibility for the sentence to be performed, understood and repeated. Thus, it is not a thesis about death. It is simply that for the sentence, spoken or written, (actually I would say 'a mark' rather than 'a statement' for reasons which will become clearer when we address the question of animality) to be understood it must be possible for its link with the origin to be interrupted.

Of course, this doesn't mean that the sentence 'I am dead' is true. I am interested in meaning not truth here. However, if you take into account this necessary possibility of my being radically absent, then, in a certain way, it *is* true that the one who is saying this is, as structurally absent, 'dead'. That is, in a certain way, the sentence is *also* true, only not at the same level. Whether it is fatal or not doesn't matter – in this case death is structurally implied in the *functioning* of the sentence.

Incidentally, that is why the second quote that you make refers to 'functioning', as well as the quote at the end about animality. As a conceptual philosopher I am analyzing the function of a sentence. The *Bedeutung* of 'I am alive', for instance, is possible only if it is not impaired by falsity. That is, only if I *can* be dead at the moment when it is functioning can the sentence be possible or intelligible. That is all. And that is why the discussion has nothing to do with a metaphysics of life/death, or of mortality/immortality. It is a philosophical, conceptual analysis of the functioning of a sentence.

I want to turn these points towards your references to Platonism. As I say, the fact that meaning can survive death does not mean that I have to die for my sentence to be meaningful. What is important is that it can survive. And everyone knows that every mark can survive them. If I make a mark (even a meaningless mark) on the page, I know at that moment that it can survive me. Even if I am immortal, it can survive me, it can function without me. Now you say: 'The fact that meaning can survive...connects with a different element in Rousseau's thought which Derrida rightly identifies as Platonist.' Well this is a very complicated problem, all the more so because it is closely linked to my debt to Husserl's analysis of idealization. First of all, as you know, Husserl is critical of Plato. When he speaks of the 'idea' or the 'ideal' or 'idealization', he distinguishes himself from any Platonism. Furthermore, it is true, I am very interested in and indebted to Husserl's analysis of idealization. One could say that I 'borrow' from him while leaving him at a certain point, and what I borrow from him is the analysis of what he calls 'idealization'. What, then, is idealization according to Husserl? Let us take for example a word – or, as I would rather say, a mark. For a mark to *be* a mark, to be perceived and understood and interpreted as a mark, it has to be repeatable, it has to be *iterable*, as 'the same' mark. This explains why every mark, everything I say or write (for example, Poe's sentence), can survive me. The sentence, to be a sentence, must be repeatable as 'the same'. Equally, if I identify it as 'the same' I have to admit that it is repeatable, it can be repeated another time and without me. This is what it means to say that the sentence is an ideality, an ideality which is distinct from *any* occurrences actually made at some point. We can publish this book by Poe a million times, I can repeat this sentence a million times, and it will remain 'the same'. And this sameness is ideal: it is an ideal object. But you don't have to be a Platonist or a transcendentalist to say this. On the contrary, if you take an interest, as Husserl does and as I try to do in my own way, in the *process* of idealization, that is in the *history* of ideal objects or ideas, then, if you understand Platonism as the view that ideas are 'present in the sky' or, as it were, just 'fall from the sky', you are not a Platonist.

Husserl was deeply interested in the history of ideas, the history of idealization, the history of objective truth, even the history of the transcendental ego. So, in that sense, I don't want to suggest that Husserl's analysis of idealization was Platonist. Thus I do not accept that 'only a being similarly freed from the contingencies of space and time could grasp transcendental meanings of this kind'. I don't think these are 'transcendental meanings', and when I say what you recall there, I am not acting as a transcendental philosopher.

You go on to say that 'such a being, as Plato famously argued in the *Phaedo*, must be immortal. But we know that we are not immortal.' Well, okay, perhaps we are not immortal. But, again, this is not the point, and things are not so simple. The gesture I make when I idealize an object is a way of producing and organizing a survival which may be, *in principle*, endless. In a certain way, language *is*, in its structure, 'immortal'. That's what idealizing means. We may be mortal, but since language is not embodied in *any* particular empirical body, it is, in its ideal structure, in its nature, 'immortal'. Thus, *in principle*, the sentence in the book by Poe, since it is structurally distinct from *any* copies, *any* exemplar, *any* occurrence or repetition, *could* 'not die'. Again, this is not to say it will not die, but that it is structured in such a way that it is 'immortal'.

Now, let me add that in my introduction to Husserl's *The Origin of Geometry*, and elsewhere, I have also raised critical questions about this point. I cannot reconstitute it all here, but I want to emphasize that I am also suspicious about this notion of 'eternity'. What I am analyzing here is the 'eternal' solely as the structure or meaning of an ideal object. But, as you know, Husserl speaks of the *absolute* ideal object, what he calls a 'free' or 'unbound' ideal object (specifically a mathematical object) which is 'eternal' in a more problematic way. Nevertheless, we might still say that the ideal object, is 'immortal' – only, *pace* Husserl, that doesn't mean that it won't die.

I can develop this by connecting my remarks to the theme of finitude. You say: 'My first question then is just why we should assent to this being a phenomenon of finitude. I raise this question not just for its own sake but because of its role in the context in which I first raised it; namely, Derrida's rejection of Platonism and indeed, his rejection of metaphysics in general'. First of all, while I have indeed written that 'infinite *différance* is finite' – and this notion of 'infinite *différance*' relates directly to Husserl's analysis of idealization and the writings by me on Husserl I have just mentioned – this is not a thesis about mortality or about the finitude of a subject or of a human being either. Rather, it refers to the internal structure of teleology that we spoke about this morning. And just in passing, since you mention in the same sentence my so-called 'rejection' of metaphysics, I have insisted again and again that I am not 'rejecting' metaphysics. I do not 'reject' metaphysics. Not even Platonism. Indeed, I think there is an unavoidable necessity of re-constituting a certain Platonic gesture. For example, what I said a moment ago about idealization was in a certain way true to a certain Plato. So that is not my 'style', the 'style' of my relationship to the tradition: I am not 'rejecting' anything, certainly not metaphysics and certainly not Plato.

Moving on, I come now to the question of the private/public distinction. Of course, again, I have to confess that I'm not familiar with Wittgenstein. That is a problem, and I can't address it here. But as to what you call the similarities between Wittgenstein's private language argument and what I say about absence, I will simply say this (without objecting to Wittgenstein but trying to justify my own non-reference to the private/public distinction.) This distinction, taken literally, has an enormous history, an enormous political history, cultural history, and I wouldn't use it lightly. I would certainly say that *différance*, is, let's say, a *limit* to interiorisation, to intimacy, to the inside – so that when you take into account the necessity of *différance* you have no pure interiorty, no pure inside. However, I wouldn't call this inside 'private' for the reasons I gave a moment ago, and I wouldn't call the outside 'public' either. Nevertheless, perhaps what I am saying is in agreement with the spirit of Wittgenstein's analysis. Wherever *différance* is at work – and that is *everywhere* – every re-appropriation 'inside' encounters a limit. So there is no pure 'inside' everywhere there is *différance*. That, by the way, is why one cannot simply speak of 'human language' either, but only of marks or traces which hold also for animals. Still a trace is immediately *not* 'private'. In the structure of the trace you have something that perhaps Wittgenstein would call 'public', but that I would simply call 'beyond my absolute re-appropriation': it is left outside, it is heterogeneous and it is outside. In short, then, perhaps there is here a possible link with Wittgenstein, but it will have to be reconstructed around the history of these notions of 'private' and 'public', and I am too concerned with and interested in politics and history to use them so easily.

Now the next question, again a very difficult one, has to do with the distinction between the other and time, between alterity, intersubjectivity and time. Again, you make recourse to Wittgenstein in a way which I cannot address here. I quote you: 'If one thinks back to the Wittgensteinian debates again, it is clear that there are substantive issues concerning the alleged normativity of meaning and the role of a community in sustaining the practice of a language-game which involves other minds rather more than other times.' I would immediately agree on the level of the normativity of meaning. No doubt, for a meaning to be understood and for discussion to start, for literature to be read, we need a community that has, even if there are conflicts, a certain desire for normativity, and so for the stabilization of meaning, of grammar, rhetoric, logic, semantics and so on. (But, by the way, if these imply a community, I wouldn't call it a community of 'minds' for a number of reasons – not least those touched on in response to your last question regarding the 'inner'.) This is obvious. And, again, I would say that it is true even for animals, for animal societies. They form a community of interpretation. They need that. And some normativity. There is here some 'symbolic culture'.

But this is not really the context in which I connect the question about the other who is 'radically other' (that is, is another 'origin of the world', another 'ego' if you want, or another 'zero point of perception') with that of 'another moment' in time (between this now and the other now, the past now and the now to come, there is an absolute alterity, each now is absolutely 'other'). So how do I connect the question of the constitution of time (and the alterity within the living present) and the question of the other (of the 'alter ego' as Husserl would say)? Well my quick answer would be that the two alterities are indisociable. A living being – whether a human being or an animal being – could not have any relation to another being as such without this alterity in time, without, that is, memory, anticipation, this strange sense (I hesitate to call it knowledge) that every now, every instant is radically other and nevertheless in the same form of the now. Equally, there is no 'I' without the sense as well that everyone other than me is radically other yet also able to say 'I', that there is nothing more heterogeneous than every 'I' and nevertheless there is nothing more universal than the 'I'.

Simon Glendinning: I am sorry to intervene so abruptly, but we are running short of time and we are only just coming to the end of question 2. What shall we do?

Jacques Derrida: How much time do we have left?

Simon Glendinning: You could take another five minutes or so responding to Tom.

Jacques Derrida: Well, then, let me select two points in a rather messy way. First, Sartre. Now, I've nothing against Sartre as you know. He was part of my family! But we don't need Sartre to speak of the 'for itself'. You say I am speaking through the voice of Jean-Paul Sartre when I speak about autoaffection and the for-itself. What you call 'the old war-horse'. No! You speak at this point of 'ancestry' – and I am always an heir and very grateful to my ancestors and fathers and professors and so on – but here I do not need Sartre. I have other references! Hegel, Heidegger... I do not need Sartre!

Second, on the question of the 'quasi' of transcendentality. If we had time I would insist on my difficult and uneasy (uneasy for myself) strategy with the 'quasi'. I present myself as someone as suspicious as you as to the distinction between the transcendental and the empirical. But at the same time, being true to Husserl and to other philosophers, trying to avoid empiricism – a certain form of empiricism – I speak of an ultra-transcendentalism. So I am not a transcendentalist: I am an ultra-transcendentalist or a quasi-transcendentalist. But explaining this would really require a long time.

Simon Glendinning: Okay, well since we only have a minute or two left before we should turn to Stephen Mulhall's presentation, I wonder if I could just ask you quickly to respond to the question about animal life.

Jacques Derrida: Well, if I had to isolate a point of real misunderstanding that would be on the question of 'the animal'. No, Tom, from the very beginning I took your side on this question. As I have indicated already, when I referred to 'trace' rather than to 'human language' in the deconstruction of logocentrism, it was already my quite deliberate aim to free the space for another discourse on 'the animal'. For me, from the start, the structure of '*différance*' holds for the animal too, 'trace' holds for the animal too. So from the very beginning I was against the Cartesian attitude towards animality, from the very beginning. You mentioned the more recent text *Of Spirit*, but you did not mention (and should have mentioned!) that it has a very organized and deliberate *critique* of Heidegger on animality. I am constantly critical of Heidegger's concept of animality. Indeed, I have often said that if you want to locate the trace of phonocentrism and logocentrism (and metaphysics if you want) in a philosopher, look at what he says about 'the animal'. The animal is for me a fundamental problem, and I am on your side Tom! So I am all the more surprised that you neglected these things. More recently still, I devoted a long text (part of which has been published) in which I – let us say 'deconstruct' to save time! – in which I deconstruct not only Descartes but many others who, consciously or unconsciously, have followed Descartes up to now (and that includes Kant, Lacan and Levinas, as well as Heidegger.) I have tried to address, to deconstruct, the prevailing discourse on animality dominant today in humanity. And it is not only a discourse: it is a politics, it is a practice, it is a general organization of human society. So that is why this point really surprised me more than any others in your talk. That is why I was insolent enough to ask you to read the whole quote about the concept of animality when you were speaking. Let me read it again: 'If we consider the *concept* of animality not in its content of understanding or misunderstanding but in its specific *function*…' You see, here I am analyzing the functioning of this concept in metaphysical discourse. It is not *my* assumption, it is not *my* discourse. It is the way people, philosophers, refer to animality, to life. For me *life is différance*. Or again, what *I* say about *différance* is true also for what *they* call 'the animal'. And let me add that in the text which has just been published, I even refuse to speak of 'the animal' in general. For as soon as you speak of 'the

animal' – as if there was this thing, 'the animal', as a homoge-
neous generality – you have already accepted all the presuppositions of metaphysics. I would never speak of 'the animal'. I don't
think there is such a thing as 'the animal'. So that's why I would
disagree with you, Tom, at least on that point.
Simon Glendinning: We will have to leave it there, I am afraid.
Maybe we can come back to the idea of the 'singular individual'
later.
Jacques Derrida: Yes, yes, simply I don't oppose substitution to
singularity. It's the same thing!
Simon Glendinning: Well, thank you very much for those
responses. Now I think we can move straight on to Stephen
Mulhall who will give a slightly shorter presentation, which, as I
said at the start, really involves only one question.

WITTGENSTEIN AND DECONSTRUCTION

Stephen Mulhall

My question for Derrida can be posed very directly. Why, in the
course of your writings, have you never engaged in any detailed
consideration of Wittgenstein's *Philosophical Investigations*?

I ask this question, despite being aware that not even a writer
of your productivity can hope to address every text in the history
of philosophy in which he might have an interest, because the
highly distinctive prose of the *Investigations* appears to me to pose
in an unusually powerful way at once an invitation and a challenge to what one might call deconstructive reading.

If I were to say that Wittgenstein's writing in this book might
well be described as 'patient, open, aporetical, in constant transformation, often more fruitful in the acknowledgement of its
impasses than its positions', you might recognize the citation of
words you used to characterize those aspects of the work of
J.L. Austin which attracted you sufficiently to devote an essay to
certain parts of it (Derrida 1988, p. 14). You might then appreciate that one way of thinking of my question is as an invitation to
imagine a deconstructive reading of the *Investigations* as a new
direction for the exploration of what is often called ordinary
language philosophy that you began in the three essays collected
in *Limited Inc.*

I am well aware that this way of casting my invitation is not at first likely to seem appealing; the Afterword to *Limited Inc* makes it abundantly clear just how disturbing you found the polemical tone, and the attendant lapses of scholarly integrity, of the exchanges with Searle that followed upon the publication of 'Signature Event Context' (just as the absence from the volume of Searle's reply to that essay makes it clear that he feels no less disturbed, and no doubt for what he takes to be similar reasons). I do not, however, doubt that you are capable of distinguishing between your interest in Austin's work and your interest in Searle's, and of acknowledging not only that the species of ordinary language philosophy represented by Austin can be inherited in ways other than that of Searle, but also that there is another species of ordinary language philosophy than that represented by Austin, and hence another way of attempting to make the idea of the ordinary (with respect to language and to life) philosophically fruitful. Stanley Cavell's recent essay 'Counter-Philosophy and the Pawn of Voice' (in Cavell 1994), represents the former possibility; it describes itself as pretending that your controversy with Searle did not happen, as speaking to your words on Austin as if for the first time – thereby enacting a speech-act of the very kind under discussion in your first essay in order to free it, and Austin, from a certain kind of misappropriation, and to free himself to respond to your words in ways that you may find rather more congenial, even if no less resistant. Wittgenstein's *Philosophical Investigations* represents the latter.

Re-reading those earlier essays on Austin and Searle in the light of that second possibility, the attractiveness of Wittgenstein as a further participant in the discussion they begin becomes more specifically striking. As a way of indicating this, the perhaps over-familiar words of the opening section of the *Investigations* suggest themselves. To begin with, it is worth remarking that the first words of that section, and hence of the book, are a citation of another's words – another in whom you have shown an interest elsewhere. It is also worth noting that that citational gesture embodies a certain ambiguity. On the one hand, detached from their textual and cultural context, Augustine's words can appear utterly unremarkable to readers accustomed to contextualize Wittgenstein's text as inheriting the philosophical tradition of Frege and Russell, and hence can make Wittgenstein's citation of them appear utterly remarkable. Why, one might say, choose to cite a handful of sentences relating Augustine's brief and apparently casual reminiscences of an early stage of his initiation into language, rather than sentences from other authors (perhaps even other sentences from the same author) whose interest in language is more self-evidently philosophical or philosophically relevant? So taken, Wittgenstein's gesture questions this sense of self-evidence, implying that, if these words of Augustine require a philosophical response from him, then we cannot say in advance that any uses of words – and hence any aspects of human culture and experience – are beyond (his conception of) philosophy's interest.

On the other hand, the very act of citing a passage from another's text necessarily points one's reader towards the uncited remainder of that text; encountering those words in their new context thereby invites us to reconsider the relation between them and their old context. So taken, Wittgenstein's gesture might be taken to ask whether the first nine books of the *Confessions* (from the first of which the cited sentences come) can rightly be assumed to form a self-evidently non-philosophical prologue to its concluding four self-evidently philosophical books, or whether such a dichotomous characterisation would misrepresent the structure of their original context, which might rather be taken (for example) as implying that Augustine's culminating metaphysical questions are invited or even made unavoidable by his autobiographical exercises. Their citation might then imply that Wittgenstein similarly envisages the autobiographical as tending towards the philosophical, that he has an interest in (at least one version of) the idea that the autobiographical is a means of access to, even a medium of, the philosophical. Your own remarks about the quasi-structure of iterability that underlies what you call the possibility and impossibility of citation would suggest that we need not and should not choose between these possibilities. Need we, or should we, choose to think that it was beyond Wittgenstein to have wished to make use of this effect of iterability?

Re-reading your reply to Searle's reply to 'Signature Event Context' in this context, I was particularly struck by his choice (and your re-examination) of the example of a shopping list (Derrida 1988, pp. 49–50). For of course, Wittgenstein's first response to the picture of language that he claims to read in the words of Augustine that he cites is to tell a tale involving a shopping list.

Now think of the following use of language: I send someone shopping. I give him a slip marked 'five red apples'. He takes the slip to the shopkeeper, who opens the drawer marked 'apples'; then he looks up the word 'red' in a table and finds a colour sample opposite it; then he says the series of cardinal numbers – I assume that he knows them by heart – up to the word 'five' and for each number he takes an apple of the same colour as the sample out of the drawer. – It is in these and other ways that one operates with words. (Wittgenstein 1958, §1)

It is worth remarking at once that the words Wittgenstein's shopper is operating with are written – in contrast to the words Augustine's child grapples with, which are rather spoken by his elders as they go about their own affairs. Furthermore, whereas the words in Augustine's tale co-exist with those uttering and hearing them, never quite detaching themselves from (as if reinforced or substantiated by) their presence, the words of Wittgenstein's shopper are made to function in the absence of the one who composed the shopping-list. Could there be a more apt acknowledgement of the iterability of words?

We must, however, take care to acknowledge the highly specific character of this shopping-list's narrative context. For example: I believe that it continues to be taken as self-evident that Wittgenstein means this tale to be an unquestionable invocation of our ordinary life with words, to be placed in opposition to Augustine's unquestionable misrepresentation of that life – that this shopping trip is an unremarkable and exemplary instance of what his philosophizing thinks of as ordinary language. It must not be denied that his counter-tale makes evident differences in the ways colour words, number words and nouns can be employed which are repressed in Augustine's tale. But it cannot simply be maintained that Wittgenstein's counter-tale is a paradigm of ordinariness in any simple sense. For how common or everyday an experience is it to observe someone attempting to buy appples by mutely presenting a shopping list to the shopkeeper? Is a store where the shopkeeper keeps his fruit in drawers, employs a sample chart when selecting amongst them by colour, and counts aloud as he deposits each apple in his customer's bag, one we would be inclined to call 'ordinary'? For Wittgenstein to present such a surreal episode as an unremarkable example of the way we operate with words is surely to place any simple concept of everyday human transactions under intolerable strain. But if nothing could be more extraordinary than this scene of supposedly ordinary life, what might Wittgenstein's idea of the ordinary actually amount to?

My suggestion is that the extraordinariness of this scene of shopping in fact shows that Wittgenstein conceives of the ordinary not as immune to, and hence as available as a simple counterweight to, philosophical appropriations and misappropriations, but as inherently vulnerable to them. For when his interlocutor resists his brusque assertion that the shopkeeper understands the words he operates with, the cast of her questions ('how does he know where and how he is to look up the word "red" and what he is to do with the word "five"?') implies that only answers invoking inner, mental operations underlying his behaviour could confer understanding and hence significance upon it. But such mental operations are typically imagined as internalized versions of the kind of processes of comparison and correlation that the shopkeeper goes through publicly in Wittgenstein's counter-tale; and this has a double implication.

First, it implies that the interlocutor's doubts about the shopkeeper's understanding are groundless (for if internal versions of those operations would remove her doubts, why should the publicness or externality of the operations he actually performs raise any such doubts in the first place – unless such doubts are motivated by attributing magical powers to the sheer fact of interiority?). Second, if the shopkeeper's surreal, oddly mechanical way with words amounts to an externalized representation of the way Wittgenstein's interlocutor imagines the inner life of all ordinary language-users, it thereby shows us how surreal and oddly mechanical our picture of the inner life of human beings actually is, and thus reveals itself as not so much a depiction of how Wittgenstein imagines ordinary life should be, but as a realization of what he takes to be one of our fantasies of it. And if the drawers and tables of his grocer's shop reflect the architecture and furnishings of the mental theatre we attribute to ourselves, and the robotic, chanting shopkeeper is the homunculus who occupies its stage, then if we, as readers, happily accept Wittgenstein's apparent invitation to regard this tale as an episode from ordinary life and proceed to berate his interlocutor for failing to do likewise, we are at once participating in the very confusions that we are so quick to condemn in others, and revealing the ways in which the realm of the ordinary (on Wittgenstein's conception of it) can prove vulnerable to philosophical depredations as well as providing a means of overcoming them.

So much for the shopkeeper; what, however, of the shopper? I have suggested that we do not typically think of shopping-lists as made for use as an alternative to speech; we rather think of them as more commonly employed in conjunction with further words, for example as an aide-memoire for conversational exchanges with shopkeepers. Are there, nevertheless, ways of imagining Wittgenstein's scene as ordinary or everyday? One way would be to imagine the shopper (and the elder who sent him) as mute, without the ability to speak. Since there is no necessity to think of their muteness as a loss (no need to imagine that they once possessed the capacity to speak and then were deprived of it), why should their way of using the shopping list be thought of as anything other than ordinary for them? After all, such perhaps untypical ways of operating with words can achieve their goal (the shopper will get the apples for his elder), and their success depends upon exploiting perfectly ordinary aspects of the powers of words; ordinary words, we might say, just are so made as to be usable in such ways.

There is another way of imagining Wittgenstein's scene as ordinary. For if we recall that, in its context, the tale is made to counter Augustine's tale of childhood, we might realize that Wittgenstein's words describe the situation of a child sent on an errand. (Indeed, thinking again about the fairy-tale quality of the shopkeeper's arrangements and actions, quite as if he is inhabiting a child's fantasy of a grocer's shop, we might further ask: is the child's parent actually sending him to the local store, or rather participating in a game the child is playing with a friend, one playing at being the customer and the other the shopkeeper? Other paths open up here, to be followed out elsewhere.) In effect, then, where Augustine's elders display little interest in teaching him how to speak (his tale rather suggesting that he was left to work the matter out for himself), Wittgenstein's child has elders who are fully engaged in the task of initiating him into language, and do so by encouraging the child to play a part in their life with words.

Is such a child 'really' or 'properly' buying groceries, or is he 'really' 'only' playing at doing so? Is playing at something a matter of pretending to do it, or of making believe that one is doing it (a matter of deception, or of suspending disbelief)? Is playing at shopping not really shopping (perhaps even 'in a peculiar way hollow or void . . . , language . . . used not seriously, . . . parasitic . . . [an] etiolation' (J.L. Austin, cited in Derrida 1988, p. 16))? Clearly, understanding Wittgenstein's child means taking a very different path across the field of concepts with which the debates between you, Austin, Searle and Cavell have concerned themselves. Suppose, provisionally to re-open these exchanges, we hypothesize that the child's willingness to play expresses his knowledge that he will be an adult and his desire to be an adult, that it signifies his wanting to do the things we do together with his knowledge that he can't as yet quite do them. Then we might say that playing at shopping is a serious business both for the child and for its elders; and we might further say that, according to Wittgenstein's counter-tale, inheriting language is a matter of inheriting a willingness to play with words, of acknowledging words as themselves playful.

The scope and ramifications of this idea of play with and in language are in question throughout the remainder of the *Investigations*. Even staying within the first section, however, we can say that its future elaborations are inflected by its encoding of Wittgenstein's apparent response to Augustine's portrait of the relation between language and desire. Augustine's child plainly acquires the impression that language as such is an instrument for the expression and satisfaction of desire; he depicts the world of his elders as pervaded with desire – as a realm in which human beings struggle to seek and have what they want, and to reject or avoid what they do not want. Wittgenstein's counter-tale does not exactly contest this: his child is, after all, acting as a messenger for one elder's linguistic expression of desire to another, and will presumably act as a messenger for the other's attempt to satisfy it – and one of our earliest stories (a story from the book with which Augustine ends the *Confessions* by occupying himself) links apples with desire. On the other hand, what one might call the sheer ordinariness of the adult exchange this child facilitates, its quotidian sense that the elder's investment in his desire for an apple allows for the possibility of the shopkeeper's inability to satisfy it, seems to lack the background (perhaps metaphysical, perhaps spiritual) of a world of unceasing, desirous struggle conjured up so effectively by Augustine – a world of original sinfulness delivered over to its own reproduction, as children imbibe their elders' enacted conception of words as instruments of self-satisfaction.

It is as if Wittgenstein wishes to drive a wedge between the idea of a connection between language and desire, and Augustine's idea of that connection. Since Wittgenstein's tale variously implies that the inheritance of language is emblematic of human maturation, that this inheritance depends upon the child's willingness to desire it and to use it to give expression to its own desires, and that play is its primary mode of acquisition, one might say that, for him, to acquire language is to participate in the play of human desire. But by dissociating himself from Augustine's visions of language users as submitting to the need to submit the world to their will, he also implies that human desire is distinguishable from, say, need or fixation – that the play of words can allow us to see beyond an inability to accept the world's independence from our will.

Take the evident but unacknowledged surreality of the shopkeeper as designed to reveal our capacity to take what is utterly extraordinary as ordinary, and the evident but unacknowledged familiarity of the shopper as designed to reveal our capacity to take what is ordinary as utterly extraordinary. Is this an ordinary, an everyday or familiar, notion of the ordinary? Is it Austin's? It does not seem that one can simply say of it, as you say of Austin's, that it has 'metaphysical origins' (Derrida 1988, p. 18) – at least, not without acknowledging Wittgenstein's own implicit acknowledgement that metaphysics originates in opposition to the ordinary, and hence is always already capable of occluding or marking it. How, then, might one proceed with a deconstructive reading of a text which persists in seeing instruction for philosophy in the concept of the ordinary despite or beyond such an acknowledgement of its equivocations?

DERRIDA'S RESPONSE TO MULHALL

Simon Glendinning: Thank you Stephen for that fascinating reading of the opening of the *Investigations*. I don't know how you want to play this Professor Derrida?

Jacques Derrida: It is difficult! I won't go back to my 'problem' with Wittgenstein. Perhaps one day I will 'solve' it in some way, but not today. To begin with let me just say that I think one of the most important things in your paper, Stephen, was to do with the problem of 'inheriting language'. And I think I was in full agreement with everything you said on that point. On the question of 'ordinary language' on the other hand – which is, I think, the central issue in your discussion – I am still suspicious. However, when I say I am suspicious of this concept it is not because I think that there is *something else* than ordinary language. I am suspicious of the *opposition* between ordinary/extraordinary language. What I am trying to do is to find – and I think this is close to the Wittgenstein that you presented – the production of the extraordinary *within* the ordinary, and the way the ordinary is, as you put it, 'vulnerable' to or not 'immune' to what we understand as extraordinary.

In a minute I will try to develop this a little further with respect to Austin, and from the point of view of another text by Austin. But first, I would just like to add a word or two to what you said about Wittgenstein's shopping scene. Don't you think that what Wittgenstein is describing here (and the scene is not so 'ordinary', as you rightly said) is a sort of 'machinery' or 'technique'? Not simply a 'mental operation', but an operation – Wittgenstein speaks of 'operating with words' – perhaps like a computer. To me what this description highlights is the installation of a certain 'technology', *through iterability*, within our mental operations. So what you call 'magical' here, attributing magical powers to the sheer fact of iterability, these magical powers are simply the technology which is implied in arithmetic, in calculation, in grammar, in semantics, and so on. So I was struck by the technological aspect of this description. As if Wittgenstein was describing this series of operations as machine-like operations within the inner life, a description which would imply that a certain '*techne*' is already at work *within* the so-called 'private' or 'inner' sphere of mental operations.

Of course, now more than ever we can be tempted by the model of the computer when we try to analyze what we are doing when we speak and we count. It seems that, like computers, we are just 'running', like a mechanism. But, in the 'running' supposed by iterability, '*techne*' is not simply opposed to the possibility of a non-mechanical decision. Indeed it is its very chance. A chance that therefore entails the greatest risk, even the menace of 'radical evil'. Otherwise, that of which it is the chance would not be 'the leap' beyond knowledge I spoke of in the last session but just a programmed effect implying a predictability or a pure know-how, which would be the annihilation of every responsibility.

But back to Austin. I do not remember exactly, but I am sure I did say that his reference to the ordinary had metaphysical origins. However, I do not think that what I had in mind was simply the reference to ordinary language. For me *there is only ordinary language* – philosophy too is 'ordinary language'. But, since there is no opposed term here, since 'there is only ordinary language', this concept is empty. The reference is to something which is simply an open space for transformation. Thus it is on the question of the delimitation of 'ordinary language' that the issue of 'metaphysics' and 'metaphysical origins' arises.

Let me develop this very briefly by recalling Austin's text 'A Plea for Excuses' which I re-read recently – it is a wonderful text. The status of his title is particularly interesting and difficult to establish. Is he simply mentioning his subject matter, or is he also already using these words? The very beginning of this paper goes like this: 'The subject of this paper, *Excuses*, is one not to be treated but only to be introduced within such limits' (Austin 1979, p. 175). Which means that, at the beginning, he is apologizing for not treating the 'subject' of his lecture. So 'a plea for excuses' is also a description of what he is going to do, no less than the subject of a possible lecture. So how does this title function? Is it the description of a coming lecture, of a philosophical discourse on excuses, or simply the description of what this man is doing; namely, apologizing? I apologize, please excuse me, I won't be able to address the question of excuses.

Well, it is in this text, with this title, that he says he wants to insist that 'ordinary language' is not the 'last word' but is the 'first word' (*ibid.*, p. 185). It is not the last word because, he says, 'it can everywhere be supplemented and improved upon, and superseded' (*ibid.*). It can be replaced – but he adds: 'Only remember, it *is* the *first* word' (*ibid.*). So it is not the last word but it is the first word. What does that mean? In the beginning there is ordinary language – then we can, of course, supersede, improve, supplement it through a number of extraordinary languages, such as, for instance, the use of this title, 'A Plea for Excuses', which is not an 'ordinary' use of language. (Indeed, a title is never 'ordinary' ordinary language.) So this subtlety, this irony, is part of an 'ordinary language' which can always be supplanted by an extraordinary use. That is why we are to remember that it is only the first word. But now we are on a very trembling limit. On the one hand, Austin accepts that ordinary language is never pure: it can be open to substitution, artificiality, mechanicity, quotation, and so forth. On the other hand, however, when he says it is the 'first word', then with the temptation to keep to this, to maintain the purity of ordinary language, at least as the first word, then he is close to being a metaphysician. Or, again, here we have a tempta-

tion towards a delimitation of the ordinary which is 'metaphysical'. (Finally, let me just note that it is in this extraordinary and
wonderfully ironic text that Austin adds a footnote to his remarks
about ordinary language not being 'the last word': 'And forget,
for once and for a while, that other curious question "Is it true?"'
(*ibid.*, p. 185n))

Simon Glendinning: I would like to come back to this idea that
there is only ordinary language, because I think something of
what Stephen was saying was sympathetic to this claim. Isn't he
saying that the ordinary is that which constantly invites or incites
a distinctive 'metaphysical' interpretation? And that contrast is
one which, it seems to me, is very important in the arguments
about possibility and impossibility which you sketched earlier
today. For unless it is to be the same thing which is possible and
impossible we need a contrast here. Don't we want to say that the
conditions which makes some *x*, let us say 'meaning', *possible* in
actuality is at the same time what makes it *impossible* as the kind of
pure ideality which we, as 'metaphysicians' as it were, are
constantly tempted to suppose? So we do have a contrast built
into your argument there. And it seems essential to it, because
otherwise we are left with no room to distinguish something like
'meaning' in actuality from an impossible 'metaphysical' ideal.
Let me put this to you. Yes, there is only ordinary language, but
this is a language which constantly invites its own misunderstanding or idealization into some kind of ideally pure structure. We
now have just the kind of contrast that Stephen was looking for
between ordinary language and a metaphysical interpretation.

Jacques Derrida: I don't know if I am answering your question,
but if I never use the concept of ordinary language in my name
– I just quote it or borrow it – it is because I do not see a radical
and necessary opposition (and I am not against oppositions and
distinctions as such) between the ordinary and the extraordinary. This does not mean that, for me, all language is 'simply'
ordinary. While I think there is nothing else but ordinary
language, I also think that there are miracles, that what I said
about the impossible implies the constant call for the extraordinary. Take, for example, trusting someone, believing someone.
This is part of the most ordinary experience of language. When
I speak to someone and say 'Believe me', that is part of everyday
language. And yet in this 'Believe me' there is a call for the most
extraordinary. To trust someone, to believe, is an act of faith
which is totally heterogeneous to proof, totally heterogeneous to

perception. It is the emergence, the appearance in language, of
something which resists anything simply ordinary. So, while I am
not against distinctions, I cannot rely on the concept of 'ordinary
language'.
Simon Glendinning: Thank you. And that is all we have time for
I am afraid. In closing I would just like to thank all the participants who have made today so interesting and enjoyable, and of
course a special thanks to Jacques Derrida for his most generous
and stimulating contributions to the day's discussions.

References

Austin, J. L. (1979). *Philosophical Papers*, Oxford: Oxford University Press.
Cavell, Stanley (1994). *A Pitch of Philosophy*, Cambridge, Mass.: Harvard University Press.
Derrida, Jacques (1973). *Speech and Phenomena*, trans. D.B. Allison, Evanston: Northwestern University Press.
Derrida, Jacques (1974). *Of Grammatology*, trans. G.C. Spivak, Baltimore: Johns Hopkins University Press.
Derrida, Jacques (1989). *Of Spirit: Heidegger and the Question*, trans. G. Bennington and R. Bowlby, Chicago: University of Chicago Press.
Derrida, Jacques (1995). *The Gift of Death*, trans. D. Wills, Chicago: University of Chicago Press.
Hegel, G.W.F. (1977). *Phenomenology of Spirit*, trans. A.V. Miller, Oxford: OUP.
Heidegger, Martin (1993). *Basic Writings*, ed. D. Farrell Krell, London: Routledge.
Sartre, Jean-Paul (1958). *Being and Nothingness*, London: Methuen, trans. H. Barnes.
Sartre, Jean-Paul (1989). *Existentialism and Humanism*, trans. P. Mairet, London: Methuen.
Williams, Bernard (1978). *Descartes: The Project of Pure Inquiry*, Harmondsworth: Penguin.
Wittgenstein, Ludwig (1958). *Philosophical Investigations*, trans. G.E.M. Anscombe, Oxford: Blackwell.

THE READING AFFAIR:
ON WHY PHILOSOPHY IS NOT "'PHILOSOPHICAL"
THROUGH AND THROUGH'

Darren Sheppard

The purpose of the following discussion is to examine a fundamental misconception that continues to stymie much of the
reception of Jacques Derrida's texts. It concerns the question of
the relationship between deconstruction – the term that I will use
to describe 'what Derrida does' – and philosophy. It is commonly
supposed that deconstruction constitutes a distinctive 'style' of
theoretical inquiry; one that is 'other than' philosophy in the
radical sense that it rejects the norms of traditional philosophical
discourse. Against that reading, I will contend that deconstruction does not *reject* those norms but is an eminently philosophical
attempt to render an account of them. It will be argued that
deconstruction is 'other than' philosophy only in so far as, on
Derrida's analysis, philosophy is already other than it conceives
itself to be.

I

In his response to A.W. Moore, Derrida makes the following
remark: 'Although I am professionally a philosopher,' he says,
'everything I do is *something else* than philosophy. No doubt it is
about philosophy, but it is not simply "philosophical" through and
through.'[1] *Something else* than philosophy? *About* philosophy, yet
not simply 'philosophical' through and through? In my own 'more
or less fictional' construction of the situation,[2] I imagine that it is
precisely remarks such as these that continue to bemuse many of
Derrida's fellow 'professionals' within the analytic tradition. How,
I imagine them asking, is it possible to converse with a self-
declared philosopher who nevertheless appears to exempt himself
from any commitment to the norms of philosophical discourse?
To charge a philosopher who aspires to be 'philosophical through

---

[1] Above, p. 83.
[2] Cf. Geoffrey Bennington's opening remarks, above p. 35.

and through' with, for example, drawing a false inference or with breaking the law of non-contradiction, is a relatively straightforward matter. If there is disagreement, then it is most likely to be over the proper observance of such norms. But how is one to converse with a philosopher who professes to be doing '*something else* than philosophy'? Faced with the charge of having breached the law of non-contradiction or of drawing a false inference, cannot Derrida 'legitimately' claim that, since his work is 'not simply "philosophical" through and through,' the proprieties of philosophical discourse do not necessarily apply?

Whilst not articulated in such incredulous tones, a similar concern with Derrida's procedure would seem to inform some of Thomas Baldwin's remarks. Citing Derrida's claim in *Of Grammatology* regarding 'the impossibility of formulating the movement of supplementarity within classical logic, within the logic of identity,'[3] Baldwin draws a parallel between Derrida's notion of *différance* and Sartre's notion of the 'for-itself.' 'In particular,' Baldwin maintains, 'Derrida seems to have adopted one of the most problematic features of Sartre's metaphysics, namely the thesis that the principle of 'identity' (or non-contradiction) is a principle with only a limited area of application; so that there is another area – which Sartre will call 'consciousness' and Derrida 'supplementarity'(or perhaps even grammatology itself), which can somehow evade the logic of non-contradiction.' He then expresses his reservations concerning this thesis: 'these are claims with which I have little antecedent sympathy and patience,' Baldwin says. 'The limits of logic are the limits, not just of the world, but also of good sense,...and contradiction is not a condition to be embraced as if it provides a mode of being superior to the mundane logic of mere common sense.' This in turn raises the following question: 'what can be said concerning *différance*,' he asks, 'if . . . its transcendental status excludes it from ordinary logic and thus good sense?'[4]

Baldwin's suspicion would appear to be that, in the name of the-concept-that-is-not-a-concept *différance* and the notion of supplementarity, Derrida seeks to locate his practice 'beyond' the jurisdiction of the law of non-contradiction. Thus understood, one can appreciate the concern: how indeed is one to engage

[3] Jacques Derrida, *Of Grammatology*, trans. G. Spivak (Baltimore: John Hopkins University Press, 1976), 314, cited by Baldwin p. 392.
[4] Above, p. 94.

with a philosopher who considers his thought to inhabit a realm 'superior to the mundane logic of mere common sense'? Is the possibility of a properly philosophical engagement with such a 'philosopher' not already precluded?

Derrida's response is ambiguous. Taking up Baldwin's reference to the transcendental, Derrida insists that he is 'as suspicious as [Baldwin] as to the distinction between the transcendental and the empirical. But at the same time,' he continues, 'being true to Husserl and to other philosophers, trying to avoid empiricism – a certain form of empiricism – I speak of an ultra-transcendentalism. So I am not a transcendentalist: I am an ultra-transcendentalist or a quasi-transcendentalist.'[5] Hence Derrida counters the claim that the 'transcendental status' of *différance* excludes it 'from ordinary logic and thus good sense' with the suggestion that, rather than 'transcendental,' *différance* is '*ultra*-transcendental.' However, this does nothing to allay Baldwin's principal concern. Indeed it newly substantiates it. Derrida's claim that *différance* is an '*ultra*-transcendental' concept does suggest something which is 'not transcendental'; but only in so far as it is to be located 'beyond' not only the distinction between the transcendental and the empirical, but 'beyond' 'ordinary [that is, oppositional] logic' *as such*.

Yet Derrida immediately qualifies this description with another: '*quasi*-transcendentalist.' This alone should cause us to re-examine our initial interpretation of Derrida's response. For if the two prefixes are more or less synonymous – as Derrida says, 'ultra-transcendentalist *or* quasi-transcendentalist' – then 'ultra-' cannot *simply* mean that which is 'beyond.' The term '*quasi*-transcendentalist' complicates matters considerably with the idea of what is not so much '*beyond*' the transcendental as 'not quite' transcendental, or not transcendental 'through and through.' Of course, precisely what sense, if any, can be given to the notion of the 'quasi-' transcendental is not yet determined. Nevertheless, in order to understand Derrida's reply to Baldwin it is clear that an account of it needs to be given.

On the day Derrida did not provide such an account. This is especially unfortunate since it is precisely a misunderstanding over the 'ultra-' or 'quasi-' transcendental status of deconstruction – that is, over the precise sense in which it is 'not "philosophical" through and through' – that constitutes the

[5] Above, p. 107.

'fundamental misconception' I referred to earlier. Stated boldly, what Derrida has written elsewhere suggests that the 'quasi-transcendental' – and, by extension, 'quasi-philosophical' – status of deconstruction does not mean that it inhabits a place 'outside' the remit of the law of non-contradiction in the manner described by Baldwin. Rather, the claim is that deconstruction is 'quasi-philosophical' only in so far as *philosophy itself* is already 'quasi-philosophical' (or again, 'not simply "philosophical" through and through'). Yet, this is not simply to re-describe philosophy as, say, *literature* (to suggest that philosophy is 'something else than philosophy' in so far as it is *in truth* merely a mode of literary discourse).[6] Rather, Derrida's argument is that this 'difference from itself' is integral to the philosophical, something that Derrida's thought seeks to 'overcome' not by locating itself in 'another area' but by affirming it as the *ineliminable aporia of philosophy as such.*

II

I will endeavour to elaborate on this claim through an examination of A.W. Moore's contribution. Moore begins by stating that his reaction to Derrida's work, 'though not the reaction of an antagonist, *is* the reaction of an outsider.'[7] To avoid describing this 'outside' in terms of the over-determined distinction between 'analytic' and 'continental' philosophy, Moore describes it as 'conceptual' philosophy, characterised as a 'style' of philosophy that 'has as its principal aim clarity of understanding and as its principal methodological tool the analysis of concepts.'[8] And he goes on to say that whilst it 'may not involve the pursuit of truth in the way in which science does,' yet 'there is an important sense . . . in which conceptual philosophy has a *commitment* to the truth. A conceptual philosopher is as beholden to eschew that which is either false or nonsensical as a scientist is.'[9] In the wake of this characterisation, Moore then asks whether, thus defined, there are any grounds for suspecting that conceptual philosophy 'fails even in its own terms' (i.e., that conceptual philosophy cannot

[6] For an influential example of this – to which Geoffrey Bennington refers in his paper – see Jürgen Habermas, *The Philosophical Discourse on Modernity: Twelve Lectures*, trans. F. Lawrence (Cam, Mass: MIT Press, 1987), esp. pp. 187–9.

[7] Above, p. 57.

[8] Above, p. 58.

[9] Above, p. 59.

ultimately be conceptual through and through). 'If so,' he adds, 'then conceptual philosophers will obviously need some way of opposing this suspicion.' Moore insists, however, that it is not with this in mind that he raises the question in the present context, rather that 'broaching the question will direct us to some important points of contact between conceptual philosophy and the work of Derrida.'[10]

Moore's introduction is significant for two reasons. First, it is important to observe the implication that, whatever Derrida's 'style' of philosophy, it is certain to be distinguishable from 'conceptual' philosophy. In particular, the implication would seem to be that Derrida does *not* have as his 'principal aim clarity of understanding,' nor does he possess a 'commitment to the truth.' The second point to note is the manner in which Moore conceives of the possibility that conceptual philosophy might 'fail even in its own terms,' namely as a *problem requiring a solution*. As he says, if there is such a suspicion, 'then conceptual philosophers will need some way of allaying [it],'[11] some way of resolving the matter, of overcoming it once and for all; so that conceptual philosophy can be conceptual through and through.

I will return to these observations in due course. Having broached the matter, Moore proceeds to outline what failure in its own terms might comprise for conceptual philosophy. It concerns, he says, the possibility that analysis of concepts will *not* lead to clarity of understanding but only further confuse. In particular, that there is something this method cannot come to terms with, namely the 'ineffable unity – of language, of reality, and of language with reality – which makes it possible to talk about anything at all.'[12] Moore cites two famous instances in which this failure is made manifest: the 'pinch of salt' that Frege asks the reader to concede him in denying that the concept of a horse is a concept;[13] and Wittgenstein's 'concession' that certain questions regarding how thought relates to the world need to be 'passed over in silence.'[14] Not that Frege and Wittgenstein are the only ones whose thought is 'sucked into contact with the ineffable':[15] Derrida too attempts to 'come to terms' with this matter by way of

[10] Above, p. 60.
[11] Above, p. 60.
[12] Above, p. 63.
[13] Cf. Above, p. 62.
[14] Cf. Above, p. 62.
[15] Above, p. 63.

the concept-that-is-not-a-concept *différance*. In a manner that suggests 'clear links with what each of Frege and Wittgenstein is doing,' Moore maintains that '[w]hat Derrida is drawing attention to . . . is something that can never be the subject of any truth. It is that which in some quasi-Kantian way makes possible and precedes the affirmation of any truth.'[16] Moore's point is, I believe, well made, not least in as much as what is said to be at issue is the 'quasi-Kantian' status of *différance*. Indeed, as we shall see, on Derrida's analysis there is a sense in which Moore *understates* the case in articulating this 'common family of concerns.' However, Moore then asks whether, in addition to a 'common *concern*,' Frege and Derrida share a 'common *predicament*': 'If Frege's truck with the concept of a horse signals the failure of conceptual philosophy,' he asks, 'does Derrida's truck with the concept of *différance* signal the failure of his style of philosophy?'[17] We have already observed that Moore's introduction contains the implicit assumption that Derrida's 'style of philosophy' does not possess the same 'commitment to the truth' as conceptual philosophy. Now this assumption is made explicit (though it is worth noting that, at this point in Moore's reading, the suggestion is that this might be an *advantage* for Derrida). For the issue of whether Frege and Derrida share not only a common 'concern' but also a common 'predicament' arises out of the possibility that Derrida's 'style' of philosophy might elude the predicament in which conceptual philosophy finds itself in so far as it 'does not treat affirmation of truth as its sole primary mode of philosophical expression.'[18]

We will consider the suggestion that Frege and Derrida share a common 'predicament' in the next section. For the moment it is important to highlight the extent to which, in making this suggestion, Moore's conception of Derrida's practice takes on a similar hue to Baldwin's. On each of their analyses there is a properly philosophical practice that proceeds within certain limits and in accordance with certain non-negotiable laws, and *then* there is the 'something else' that Derrida practices; a process which is neither 'restricted' in this way nor beholden to the same rules. On Baldwin's account this 'something else' is described as inhabiting 'another area' beyond 'ordinary logic' and 'good sense.' On

---

[16] Above, p. 64.
[17] Above, p. 65.
[18] Above, p. 65.

Moore's account it is described as an area that 'does not labour under a restricted conception of what linguistic resources are available to it.'[19] Either way what is at issue is a practice that is quite distinct from philosophy as they wish to see it done, as they are committed to it. The question is whether this is indeed an accurate description of Derrida's project. Specifically, whether Derrida's description of what he does as 'something else than philosophy,' 'not "philosophical" through and through,' and of himself as a 'quasi-transcendentalist,' is to be taken to mean that deconstruction is 'other' than philosophy in the manner that Baldwin and Moore suggest.

Evidence that this is *not* the case – at least on Derrida's own analysis – is offered in separate remarks to Moore and to Baldwin. In response to Moore's definition of conceptual philosophy and its 'commitment to the truth' Derrida insists that he shares this commitment: 'Despite a number of appearances,' he says, 'my style has something essential to do with a motivation that one also finds in analytic philosophy.' In fact 'it is in the name of truth, of a certain truth, that I say that "*différance* is not a name nor a concept."'[20] Similarly, in response to Baldwin's remarks concerning his 'rejection of Platonism, and indeed his rejection of meta-physics in general,'[21] Derrida maintains – it is a point, he says, on which he has insisted 'again and again' – that he is 'not rejecting metaphysics. Not even Platonism. Indeed, I think there is an unavoidable necessity of re-constituting a certain Platonic gesture... So that's not my "style", the "style" of my relationship to the tradition: I am not "rejecting" anything.'[22]

What these responses have in common is an insistence that, whatever Derrida's practice is, it is *not* to be understood as 'other' than – because rejecting – a 'style' of philosophy defined in terms either of a commitment to the truth or to metaphysics. Indeed it would appear that the relation between deconstruction and philos-ophy is not to be understood in terms of a simple same/other or inside/outside relation at all. The note of frustration in his response is perhaps understandable, for Derrida has been making this point since the 1960's. As he says on one such occasion, decon-struction 'is *not* a transgression, if one understands by that a pure and simple landing into the beyond of metaphysics . . . One is

<hr>

[19]   Above, p. 64.
[20]   Above, p. 84.
[21]   Above, p. 92.
[22]   Above, p. 105.

never installed within transgression, one never lives elsewhere.' He adds: 'even in aggressions or transgressions, we are consorting with a code to which metaphysics is tied irreducibly, such that every transgressive gesture reencloses us – precisely by giving us a hold on the closure of metaphysics – within this closure.'[23] The same point is stressed again elsewhere: 'There is no sense in doing without the concepts of metaphysics in order to shake metaphysics. We have no language – no syntax and no lexicon – which is foreign to this history; we can pronounce not a single proposition which has not already had to slip into the form, the logic, and the implicit postulations of precisely what it seeks to contest.'[24]

It is quite possible, of course, that Derrida does not understand the full implications of his own practice. Nevertheless, on his account of it this much would seem to be clear: deconstruction is not 'other' than philosophy for the simple reason that, even while it is its transgression, there is no 'outside' or 'beyond' that it might inhabit. At issue, then, is a structure of inhabiting *and* not-inhabiting – of not inhabiting 'through and through' – the 'code' and 'commitments' of metaphysics or philosophy. As he says to Moore, 'I too have a commitment to the truth – *if only to question the possibility of the truth*, the history of the truth, the differences in the concept of the truth, and not taking for granted the defini-tion of truth as tied to declarative sentences.'[25] Yet if there is no language other than the language of metaphysics in terms of which this transgressive gesture might be articulated, it is equally the case that the resources of that language are not adequate to the task. The result would seem to be a rather unremarkable impasse: one cannot do without the language of metaphysics in the course of deconstructing metaphysics, but at the same time it is impossible to articulate that process in terms of the language of metaphysics. Derrida's strategy in response to this 'circle' involves, he says, a 'necessarily double gesture,'[26] that is to say, a 'single' strategy comprising two moments, one of which is intra-metaphysical and involves a commitment to the possibility of

[23] Jacques Derrida, *Positions*, trans. A. Bass (Chicago: University of Chicago Press, 1981), p. 12.
[24] Jacques Derrida, 'Structure, Sign ,and Play in the Discourse of the Human Sciences', trans. A. Bass in *Writing and Difference* (Chicago: University of Chicago Press, 1981), pp. 280–1.
[25] Above, p. 84 (emphasis added).
[26] Jacques Derrida, *Positions*, p. 6.

truth, the other of which is extra-metaphysical and involves a radical critique of the possibility of truth. As he explains:

> To 'deconstruct' philosophy, thus, would be to think – in the most faithful, interior way – the structured genealogy of philosophy's concepts, but at the same time to determine – from a certain exterior that is unqualifiable or unnameable by philosophy – what this history has been unable to dissimulate or forbid, making itself into a history by means of this somewhere motivated repression.[27]

For the moment we will leave the specifics of this 'double gesture' to one side. Suffice it to say that, on Derrida's account – and contra Baldwin and Moore – the difference between deconstruction and philosophy is not to be conceived in terms of a simple same/other or inside/outside relation. In other words, it is to be conceived in terms neither of a 'rejection' nor of an 'acceptance' of metaphysics or a commitment to the truth, but as involving *both* a moment of rejection *and* a moment of acceptance. In sum, it is to be understood as comprising a strategy that is both intra- and extra-philosophical, 'at the same time' 'faithful' and 'unfaithful' to philosophy, simultaneously committed and uncommitted to the truth.

III

This paper began with the 'more or less fictional' account of a certain sceptical response to Derrida's claim that what he does is '*something else* than philosophy'; that it is '*about* philosophy,' yet 'not simply "philosophical" through and through.' In the light of the preceding reconstruction of Derrida's account of the relation between deconstruction and philosophy, we can now provide a preliminary explanation of what this assertion might mean. Deconstruction is properly described as '*something else* than philosophy' not because it is straightforwardly 'other' but because, in addition to the 'faithful and interior' moment to which Derrida refers, deconstruction involves an 'exterior' moment that is 'unqualifiable or unnameable by philosophy.' Thus, deconstruction is in a precise sense *both* philosophical *and* non-philosophical, that is to say, 'not simply "philosophical" through and through.' And yet, I imagine my fictional sceptic querying

[27] Ibid.

whether such an account moves the debate on at all. Specifically, I imagine him or her maintaining that, far from differentiating Derrida's true position from the one falsely attributed to him by Moore and Baldwin, this explanation of the 'quasi-philosophical' status of deconstruction *attests* to the argument that Derrida's practice is 'other' than philosophy; that nothing could be *more* offensive to 'ordinary logic' and 'good sense,' and betray *less* of a 'commitment to the truth' than this 'double gesture.'

It is a criticism that requires careful consideration. To begin with the argument that the double gesture attests to the 'otherness' of deconstruction, this might indeed be the case if Derrida claimed that there is another logic 'beyond' the law of non-contradiction in terms of which the double gesture is to be articulated. It is on this point that I take issue with certain of the remarks made by Geoffrey Bennington. In his contribution, Bennington refers to the advantages of construing the relation between deconstruction and philosophy in a 'differential-but-not-oppositional way. I call this a reconstrual,' he continues, 'because it emphatically does not mean that we divide up the field into argument on the one hand and 'style' on the other . . . The 'field' here has to be thought of as differentiated in a more complex way than the more endemically territorial frontier-defined way we probably inherited from Kant.' Bennington also offers some possible resources on which such a reconstrual might draw: 'maybe fractal geometry,' he suggests, 'or something like the Australian Aboriginal understanding of space as essentially to do with lines and tracks might help.'[28]

In short, Bennington's claim would appear to be that it is possible to reconstrue the relation between deconstruction and philosophy in terms of a logic no longer bound by the law of non-contradiction (namely, one that is 'differential but not-oppositional'). On Derrida's account, however, this is to suppose we can escape the 'circle'. In other words, it is to suppose that we *do* have a language – the resources for which are perhaps to be found in fractal geometry and/or the Australian Aboriginal understanding of space – in terms of which we can articulate the relation between deconstruction and philosophy *without* '[slipping] into the form, the logic, the implicit postulations of precisely what it seeks to contest.' But this is not the case (it is, Derrida says, a naive gesture bound to fail: 'the simple practice of language ceaselessly reinstates the new terrain on the oldest ground').[29] Indeed, on this point Derrida's position is more akin to Baldwin's than to Bennington's, for as Derrida maintains that 'we cannot live elsewhere,' so Baldwin insists that 'the limits of logic are the limits, not just of the world, but also of good sense.' On Derrida's account, then, the paradoxical nature of the double gesture – the sense in which it both is and is not 'properly philosophical' – is *irreducible.* There is no 'other logic' in terms of which the logical contradiction that the double gesture constitutes might be 'ironed out,' or again, in terms of which one might make 'good sense' of it and thereby break out of the circle. Consequently, the sceptic is right – at least 'up to a point,' to borrow Bennington's phrase – when he or she declares that nothing could be *more* offensive to 'ordinary logic' and 'good sense' than the 'double gesture'; located on the border of the proper and the improper, deconstruction offends the 'good sense' of philosophy or it is nothing at all. This requires qualification, however, for it is not an offence that is local to deconstruction. Specifically, it is not to demarcate a paradoxical 'style' of philosophy (deconstruction) from a proper, non-paradoxical 'style' of philosophy ('conceptual' philosophy, for example). Rather, Derrida's fundamental claim is that the double gesture of deconstruction describes the movement of philosophy *as such.* To recall a phrase used at the very beginning of this chapter, deconstruction is only 'other' than philosophy in so far as philosophy is already other than it conceives itself to be; what it means to 'think philosophically' is *constituted* in this moment of originary transgression or 'difference-from-itself.' The moment of transgression is always already at work, even in those texts which aim to resist it, aim to stay at home – for example, in the *need* for conceptual analysis to ask for a 'pinch of salt' or acknowledge the impossibility of *complete* conceptual (expressible) analysis.

Against this background it is possible to understand the significance of Moore's question regarding whether, in addition to sharing a 'common family of concerns,' Frege and Derrida also share a 'common predicament.' For it is not simply that, in raising this issue, Moore finally makes explicit what had hitherto remained implicit regarding the 'otherness' of Derrida's practice (namely, that it neither has as its 'principal aim clarity of under-

[29] Jacques Derrida, 'The Ends of Man', trans. A. Bass in *Margins of Philosophy* (Brighton: The Harvester Press, 1982), p. 135.

standing,' nor possesses a 'commitment to the truth'). Instead it raises the question whether, for Derrida's 'style' of philosophy, 'failure even on its own terms' appears as a *problem requiring a solution.* On Moore's account the question of the intellectual probity of conceptual philosophy stands or falls on its ability to allay the suspicion that it does indeed 'fail even on its own terms,' that is to say, its ability to secure its own propriety without recourse to pinches of salt or any other such (non-philosophical) 'supplements.' What is at issue here is the possibility of complete conceptual clarification. But on Derrida's account the 'problem' of running up against an 'ineffable' residuum is not merely something that has happened to three thinkers (Frege, Wittgenstein, and Derrida). This is why it was suggested that, on Derrida's account, Moore understates the case when he identifies a 'common family of concerns' shared by these thinkers. According to Derrida, failure even on its own terms is *unavoidable* for philosophy conceived as the quest for complete conceptual clarity. The moment of ineffability that Moore locates in each of Frege's, Wittgenstein's, and Derrida's discourses, is ineliminable. Phrased otherwise, it is constitutive not of certain 'styles' of philosophy but is the condition of possibility which, in Moore's phrase, 'makes it possible to talk about anything at all.'[30] Thus, the aim of complete conceptual clarity – the complete analysis of talk about anything at all – does not just run into difficulties here or there in this or that philosopher's discourse. Rather, in order to be 'itself' every properly philosophical discourse always already contains a moment of transgression or 'supplementarity,' of *différance*, in which it draws on the resources of or depends on what it would at the same time disavow or disclaim as 'other' than itself (for example, fictions or non-logical decisions). Hence, as the condition of the *possibility* of the language of philosophy proper, *différance* names what is simultaneously the condition of *impossibility* of philosophy's proper completion. For Moore this lacuna or breach in the propriety of philosophy designates a problem to be solved, hence the idea of a 'common *predicament.*' For Derrida, on the other hand, in so far as this moment of impropriety is constitutive of philosophy as such, it designates an *aporia to be endured* (it is, Derrida says, 'an interminable experience').[31]

[30] Above, p. 63.
[31] Jacques Derrida, *Aporias*, trans. T. Dutoit (Stanford: Stanford University Press, 1993), p. 16.

However, the 'impossibility' of philosophy does not mark its end or 'death.' Rather it is an *aporia* – literally a 'non-passage' – to be affirmed. For the very same structure that interrupts the propriety of philosophy and opens it to its 'other' always also opens up the possibility for what philosophy (as such) can never anticipate. The 'other' of philosophy that is no longer *its* other. Thus opening up the possibility of the invention – the advent or 'in-coming' (*invenire*) – of what has yet to be thought. As Derrida writes:

> the most rigorous deconstruction never claimed ... to be *possible*. And I would say that deconstruction loses nothing from admitting that it is impossible;... For a deconstructive operation *possibility* would rather be the danger, the danger of becoming an available set of rule-governed procedures, methods, accessible approaches. The interest of deconstruction, of such force and desire as it may have, is a certain experience of the impossible: that is, ... of the other – the experience of the other as the invention of the impossible, in other words, of the only possible invention.[32]

Where the path or passage (*poros*) is possible, where it is simply a matter of following the rule, 'of putting into operation a determinable or determining knowledge, the consequences of some pre-established order,'[33] there is no moment of the 'invention of the other' that is not always already reinscribed within the return of the same. In the 'experience of the impossible,' on the other hand, what is at issue is the affirmation of that which exceeds the (given) possible, which 'overflows' the attempt to anticipate its arrival, to prepare a place for it within the sequence of the same. And this as the possibility of opening philosophy to a future 'beyond' the project of its own self-completion.

It is this experience of the impossible that I take Bennington to be referring to when he speaks of Derrida's 'argument with argument' by which the failure of argument to come to a properly philosophical conclusion is precisely the moment of interruption – of 'exposure' to the other – in which further argument becomes possible. For conceptual philosophy this is experienced as a

---

[32] Jacques Derrida, 'Psyché: Invention of the Other', trans. C. Porter in *Reading De Man Reading*, ed. L. Waters and W. Godzich (Minneapolis: University of Minnesota Press, 1989), p. 36.
[33] Jacques Derrida, *Aporias*, p. 17.

predicament to be overcome, for deconstruction an irreducible aporia to be affirmed. This comes out again where Derrida, in response to Stephen Mulhall, addresses the issue of ordinary language. There Derrida says that when he says he is 'suspicious' of the concept of ordinary language it is not because he thinks that 'there is something else than ordinary language.' 'What I am trying to do,' he says, 'is to find the production of the extraordinary *within* the ordinary.'[34] In other words, deconstruction does not oppose the ordinary and the extraordinary, does not oppose the logic of 'good sense' with a logic other than the logic of identity, a 'style' of philosophy that is 'liberated' from a commitment to truth. Rather it endeavours to locate the moment *within* the return of the same – *within* the 'production of the ordinary,' the possible – in which the language of philosophy is opened to its other; to the *extra*ordinary, to the (given) *im*possible.

IV

If Derrida's practice was 'other' than philosophy as Baldwin and Moore suggest, then it might indeed be pernicious in the manner that a number of critics have suggested.[35] As I have endeavoured to show, however – at least in outline – deconstruction is not in this sense 'other' than philosophy, whether the latter is defined in terms of its adherence to the law of non-contradiction or its commitment to the truth. This is not to deny that deconstruction is '*something else* than philosophy' and so 'not simply "philosophical" through and through.' Rather, it is to claim that *philosophy itself* is 'not simply "philosophical" through and through.' For Derrida, philosophy always already – at its origin – draws on the resources of that *against* which it would endeavour to define itself. Consequently, in so far as its task is to locate this constitutive impropriety, deconstruction is in a certain way rigorously philosophical, rigorously seeking the limits of conceptual clarity. Of course, whether Derrida's account of philosophy 'corresponds with the facts' is a separate question. However, in order for this debate to take place it is necessary that Derrida's position be understood. For Derrida it is not simply the discussion of his own work that is at issue: it is nothing less than the future of philosophy itself.

[34] Above, p. 117.
[35] I allude to the opening paragraph of A.W. Moore's paper, p. 57.

Notes for Contributors
The preferred length for articles in RATIO is between 5000 and 6000 words. Articles are accepted for the refereeing process on the strict understanding that they are not under consideration elsewhere. All articles submitted must be preceded by an *abstract* (maximum 200 words), and should be sent to the Editor:

Professor John Cottingham
Department of Philosophy
The University of Reading,
READING RG6 6AA, England.

Typescripts (two copies), which will not be returned, should be double spaced. To facilitate anonymous refereeing, the author's name and address should appear on a detachable title page, but nowhere else in the article. Authors of papers accepted for publication will be asked to prepare a final version (hard copy plus disk) following house style guidelines. Books for review and all other editorial correspondence should be sent direct to the Editor at the above address.

Back issues: Single issues from the current and previous three volumes are available from Blackwell Publishers Journals. Earlier issues may be obtained from Swets & Zeitlinger, Back Sets, Heereweg 347, PO Box 810, 2160 SZ Lisse, Holland.

Microform: The journal is available on microfilm (16mm or 35mm) or 105mm microfiche from the Serials Acquisitions Department, Bell & Howell Information and Learning, 300 North Zeeb Road, Ann Arbor, MI 48106, USA.

Internet: Full details of Blackwell Publishers books and journals are available on the Internet. To access use a WWW browser, such as Netscape or Mosaic, and the following URL: http://www.blackwell publishers.co.uk.

Index

affirmation of truth 63, 66–7, 68, 69
agreement, from discussion 44, 48
alterity 21, 106, 107
ambiguity 5–6, 110–11
analytical philosophy
    conceptual philosophy 75–6
    and continental philosophy
        9–10, 11, 12, 17–18
    deconstruction 41
    ordinary language 29
    philosophical history 36–7
animals
    différance 97–8, 108
    Heidegger 98, 108
    marks 103, 106
    mental life 97–8
aporia 75, 124, 132–3
arguer 36n2, 37, 48, 49
arguing 35–6
argument 35–6
    Aristotle 37
    Bennington 3n2, 133
    conclusion 45–6, 48
    deconstruction 42
    Derrida 3n2, 39, 133
    hyper-reality 47
    inheritance 11
    iterability 40
    philosophy 36–7, 45–6
    possibility/impossibility 54–5
    self-undermining 47–8
    Socrates 52
    teleology 51
    text 41–2
    Wittgenstein 46
    argutie 56
Aristotle 19, 37
aspect perception 6–7
Augustine, Saint

Confessions 111, 115
    language 111, 112–13, 115
Auseinandersetzung (explication)
    48, 49–50, 55–6
Austin, J. L.
    clarity 15
    conceptual philosophy 65–6
    Derrida on 11, 18–19, 65–6, 109
    dismantling 15–16, 17
    Gleichschaltung 13–14, 17, 31
    How to do Things with Words
        16–17, 22–3, 28
    infelicities 28–9
    inheritance 15–16
    language games 66
    locutionary acts 22
    meaning 21–2
    non-serious 31
    ordinary 116
    performative utterances 11,
        22–3, 25–6, 27–8
    'Performative Utterances' 15
    'A Plea for Excuses' 28, 118
    'Pretending' 28
    Sense and Sensibilia 13–14
    truth 26–7
auto-affection 94–5

Baldwin, Thomas 2, 79, 122, 126
Barthes, Roland 73
being-for-death 99
being-towards-death 99, 100–1
Bennington, Geoffrey 2, 8, 11, 34
    argument 3n2, 133
    reconstrual 130
    words/concepts 65

Cavell, Stanley 10, 26–7, 28, 35, 110
child's language 114–15

Cicero   37
citationality   29–30, 110–11
clarity
  Austin   15
  deconstruction   134
  Derrida   12–13, 125, 131–2
  Frege   131–2
closure   42–3
communication
  ineffable   69
  meaning-content   17, 21–2
  performative   23, 26–7, 28, 31
communication of presences   66–7
community, language games   106
computer word usage   117
concepts   7–8
  Frege   62, 65, 75, 85–6, 125,
    126
  predicates   61
  teleology   43
  words   65
conceptual philosophy
  analytical philosophy   75–6
  Austin   65–6
  context   73
  Derrida   60
  failure   62–3, 124–5, 132
  Frege   60–1, 63
  impossibility   133–4
  ineffable   63, 68–9
  language games   70–1
  Moore   9, 124–9
  science   57–8
conclusion of argument   45–6, 48
conflict   41
confrontation   18
consciousness   95
context
  conceptual philosophy   73
  deconstruction   96–7
  language games   67
  meaning   20, 21–2, 66
continental philosophy
  and analytical philosophy   9–10,
    11, 12, 17–18

Cooper, David   38
Cottingham, John   51, 52

Dancy, Jonathan   2, 81
Davidson, Donald   86, 87
death
  being-for   99
  being-towards   99, 100–1
  différance   94–7, 102
  fear of   94
  individual awareness   99
  meaning   90
  negation   94
  possibility/inevitability   102
decision   85
declarative sentences   60–1, 83
deconstruction   15–16
  analytical philosophy   41
  argument   42
  clarity   134
  context   96–7
  dialectics   42
  différance   48–9
  inhabiting/not-inhabiting   128
  non-transgressive   127–8
  philosophy   11, 40, 121–4, 127,
    129–30
  possibility   133
  reconstrual   130
  speed   51–2
  style   121
defer/deference   44, 93–4
'deferance'   94
Derrida, Jacques   2
  argument   3n2, 39, 133
  on Austin   11, 18–19, 65–6, 109
  clarity   12–13, 125, 131–2
  conceptual philosophy   60
  'Différance'   3, 63–5, 67–8, 75,
    84, 85
  Frege   131
  The Gift of Death   90, 99, 100
  Of Grammatology   45, 49, 99–100,
    101, 122
  on Heidegger   98

on Husserl   44, 67
ineffability   63–4, 75, 76–8,
    125–6
inheritance   15–16
language games   65
Limited Inc.   2–3, 109–10
'Limited Inc abc . . .'   18, 38
    non-serious   29–31
'Signature Event Context'   5,
    17–18, 19–20, 38, 65–7, 70–1,
    72, 74, 110, 111
Speech and Phenomena   89–90
Of Spirit   98, 108
'Structure, Sign and Play'   45
style   9, 38, 78–9, 105, 126
transcendentalism   95–6
truth   82–5, 132
'The White Mythology'   45
Descartes, René   97, 98, 108
desire/language   115–16
dialectics   42
différance   5, 52–3
    animals   97–8, 108
    aporia   75
    concept-that-is-not-a-concept   126
    death   94–7, 102
    deconstruction   48–9
    différence   64–5
    for-itself   95, 122
    ineffability   76–8, 81–2
    knowledge   80–2
    language   93–4, 99–100,
        105–6
    Life   108–9
    meaning   44, 92
    Moore   42
    quasi-Kantian   126
    repetitive structure   96
    supplementarity   122–3, 132
    transcendentalism   123–4
    transgression   132
    writing   5, 90–2
différence   64–5
discussion   41, 44, 48
disinheritance, philosophy   11

dismantling (Austin)   15–16, 17
Dummett, Michael   10–11, 38n5, 52

ethics
    radical evil   43, 50–1, 54
    self-undermining   47–8
    universality   100
events/utterances   21
evil   43, 50–1, 54
explication   48, 52
    see also *Auseinandersetzung*
expliquer   49–50

felicity   26–7
field concept   42–3
finitude   105
Flaubert, Gustave   46, 51–2
for-itself
    différance   95, 122
    Sartre   94–5, 107, 122
    subjectivity   94–5
force of utterances   24–5
Foucault, Michel   97
Frege, Gottlob
    clarity   131–2
    concepts   62, 65, 75, 85–6, 125,
        126
    conceptual philosophy   60–1, 63
    and Derrida   131
    Dummett on   52
    and Husserl   10–11
    'The Thought'   24–5
    truth   26, 27

Galoul, Ahmed   82
gestures, performative   84
Gleichschaltung (Austin)   13–14, 17, 31
Glendinning, Simon   35, 119
Gödel, Kurt   71
grammatology   97

Habermas, Jürgen   41, 42, 44
Hacker, P. M. S.   40
Hegel, G. W. F.
    dialectics   42

Hegel, G. W. F. (*cont.*):
  self-consciousness 93, 94
  sublation 46
  telos 43–4
Heidegger, Martin
  animals 98, 108
  Auseinandersetzung 48, 55–6
  Being and Time 98
  being-towards-death 99
  The Fundamental Concepts of Metaphysics 98
  Gleichschaltung 14
  hearing/hearkening 6
  'Letter on Humanism' 98
  understanding 4
Hobson, Marian 2
Horchen (hearkening) 6
Howells, Christina 50–1
Husserl, Edmund
  Derrida on 44, 67
  and Frege 10–11
  idealization 103–4, 105
  Kantian Idea 44
  The Origin of Geometry 104–5
  Platonism 91, 95
  signs 96
hyper-reality 47

Idea (Kant) 43, 44
ideal, philosophical 5–6, 7, 19
idealization (Husserl) 103–4, 105
identity 3, 5, 38, 95, 122
impossibility 55, 133–4
impurity of speech acts 31
inaudibility 6
individual, singular 99–102
ineffability 132
  communication 69
  conceptual philosophy 63, 68–9
  Derrida 63–4, 75, 76–8, 125–6
  différance 76–8, 81–2
  know-how/know-that distinction 79–81
  knowledge 78, 88

nonsense 74
self-stultification 68, 69
infelicities doctrine 26–7, 28–9
inheritance
  argument 11
  Austin 15–16
  Derrida 15–16
  language 116–17
  philosophy 10, 22, 32–3
intelligibility 4, 6
interpretation/reading 10–11
intersubjectivity 93–4, 106
invagination 42–3
iterability
  alterity 21
  argument 40
  identity 3, 5, 38
  language 31, 32
  marks 104
  meaning 92
  words 112, 117

justice 13

Kant, Immanuel 42
  Idea 43, 44
  transcendentalism 61
Kierkegaard, Søren 100, 101
know-how 79–81, 84
know-that 79–81
knowledge 69
  différance 80–2
  ineffability 78, 88
  language games 88
  science 57–8
  truth 77–8, 84–5

language
  Aristotle 19
  atypical usage 70, 74
  Augustine 111, 112–13, 115
  child 114–15
  desire 115–16
  différance 93–4, 99–100, 105–6
  inheritance 116–17

iterability 31, 32
muteness 114
non-serious 29–31, 67
ordinary 11, 29, 32, 91, 112–13, 116–20, 134
phonemes 3, 4
public/private 93–4, 105–6
purity 31, 118–19
thought 97
trace 94, 106, 108
see also language games
language games
Austin 66
community 106
conceptual philosophy 70–1
context 67
Derrida 65
knowledge 88
ludic objects 86–7
nonsense 67, 68
Wittgenstein 65, 115–16
life
différance 108–9
ordinary 112–14, 116
Wittgenstein 61–2
literature/philosophy 42–3, 124
locutionary acts: see speech acts
logic of presence 4, 6
logical form (Wittgenstein) 31, 63
logocentrism 40, 49, 108
logos 37, 40
ludic object language 86–7
Lyotard, J.-F. 43, 44

marks
animals 103, 106
iterability 104
statement 102–3
words 103–4
meaning
Austin 21–2
communication 17, 21–2
context 20, 21–2, 66
death 90
différance 44, 92

intentional 20–1, 23–4, 31
iterability 92
normativity 106
transcendentalism 91–2
truth 91, 103
utterances 19, 20
metalanguage 86–7
metaphor 38, 45, 46
metaphysics
analytical philosophy 76
rejected/not-rejected 105, 127
Sartre 95, 122
Moore, A. W. 2
conceptual philosophy 9, 124–9
différance 42
Points of View 57
use/mention distinction 50
More, Henry 98
Mulhall, Stephen 2, 32, 134
muteness 114

names 61, 64–5, 85
negation/death 94
non-serious language 29–31, 67
non-supplementarity 101–2
nonsense 67, 68, 74, 96
normativity/meaning 106
nouns 19

ordinary/extraordinary 112–14, 116
other/time 106–7
Oxford Philosophy 17

perception 6–7, 13–14
performativity
communication 23, 26–7, 28, 31
gestures 84
utterances 11, 22–3, 25–6, 27–8
Phillips, Dawn 87
philosophical history 36–7
philosophy
Anglo-Saxon 35–6, 39, 40–1
aporia 75, 124, 132–3
argument 36–7, 45–6

philosophy (*cont.*):
  deconstruction   11, 40, 121–4,
    127, 129–30
  inheritance   10, 22, 32–3
  literature   42–3, 124
  nonsense   96
  reconstrual   130
  stupidity   46, 51–2
  style   11, 12, 83–4
phonemes   3, 4
phonocentrism   108
Plato, *Phaedo*   92, 104
Platonism   91, 92, 95, 103, 105, 127
Poe, Edgar Allan   90, 91, 102
possibility   5, 55, 102, 133
predicate   61
presence
  communication of   66–7
  logic of   4, 6
  myth of   93–4
  possibility   5
  signs   6
private language argument   93–4,
  105–6
propositions, empirical/grammatical
  87–8
purity of language   31, 118–19
Putnam, Hilary   73

quasi-transcendentalism   107, 123–4
Quine, W. V. O.   96
Quintilian   37

ratio   54
Ratio conference   1–2, 32
ratiocination   56
reading   10–11, 39–40
Reason (Kant)   43
reconciliation   53
reconstrual   130
Roden, David   86
Rousseau, J. J.   49, 100

Sartre, Jean-Paul
  for-itself   94–5, 107, 122

Foucault on   97
metaphysics   95, 122
singular individual   101
Saussure, Ferdinand de   4
science   57–8
Searle, John
  and Austin   17, 28
  Derrida on   84
  'Reply to Derrida: Reiterating the
    Differences'   18, 70n29, 110,
    111
self   99
self-consciousness   93, 94–5
self-stultification   68, 69
sense/ambiguity   5–6
sensibility   3, 4, 6
sentences   24–5
  declarative   60–1, 83
  indicative   24–5, 26
shopping list examples   111–12, 117
sign   6, 7, 45, 91, 96
signified   70–1, 95
signifier   70–1, 91
sin   100–1
Socrates   52
solliciter   49
speech acts   22
  eventuality/possibility   29, 30–1
  impurity   31
  inaudibility   6
  see also utterances; words
Spivak, G. C.   49
statements   22–3, 102–3
Stratton-Lake, Philip   47–8
stupidity   46, 51–2
style
  deconstruction   121
  Derrida   9, 38, 78–9, 105, 126
  philosophy   11, 12, 83–4
subjectivity   94–5
  intersubjectivity   93–4, 106
substitution   102
suicide   82–3
supplementarity   94, 95, 100, 122–3,
  132

teleology 43, 44, 51, 54, 105
telos (Hegel) 43–4
temporalization 93–4
testimony 85
text
 argument 41–2
 deconstruction 15–16
 field 43
thought 97, 125
time 93–4, 106–7
token/type 86–7
trace 94, 106, 108
transcendentalism
 Derrida 95–6
 différance 123–4
 Kant 61
 meaning 91–2
 quasi-transcendentalism 107,
  123–4
 ultra-transcendentalism 107,
  123–4
transgression 127–8, 132
translation 48, 49, 55
Travis, Charles 20
truth
 affirmation 63, 66–7, 68, 69
 Austin 26–7
 commitment 84–5, 124, 125, 126,
  128, 132
 declarative sentences 83
 Derrida 82–5, 132
 felicity 26–7
 Frege 26, 27
 knowledge 77–8, 84–5
 meaning 91, 103
 science 57–8
 testimony 85
type/token 86–7

ultra-transcendentalism 107, 123–4
understanding 4

use/mention distinction 50, 70–3,
 87–8
utterances
 events 21
 force 24–5
 meaning 19, 20
 non-citational 29–30
 performative 11, 22–3, 25–6,
  27–8
 serious/non-serious 28, 29

Williams, Bernard 10, 11, 12, 98
Wittgenstein, Ludwig
 argument 46
 aspect perception 6–7
 empirical/grammatical
  propositions 87–8
 language/desire 115–16
 language games 65, 115–16
 logical form 31, 63
 ordinary life 112–14
 Philosophical Investigations 5–6, 96,
  109, 110, 115
 private language argument 93–4,
  105–6
 problem of life 61–2
 shopping lists 111–12, 117
 thought 125
 Tractatus 67, 96
Woehrling, Eric 48–9
words
 computers 117
 concepts 65
 iterability 112, 117
 marks 103–4
 use/mention distinction 50,
  70–3, 87–8
 see also language; language games;
  speech acts
writing
 différance 5, 90–2
 sensibility 4

Printed and bound by CPI Group (UK) Ltd, Croydon, CR0 4YY

09/06/2025

14686120-0001